C Tiaras

The power of childlikeness

Marvin K. Lucas

Capes and Tiaras—The Power of Childlikeness
© 2015 by Marvin K. Lucas

Printed in the United States of America.

ISBN: 978-1-939086-99-0.

Unless otherwise indicated, all Scripture references are from the Holy Bible, New International Version, copyright 1973, 1978, 1984, 2011 by the International Bible Society. Used by permission of Zondervan Bible Publishers.

Cover design: Josie Miller

Interior design: Toney Mulhollan

Copy editor: Amy Morgan.

Illumination Publishers is committed to caring wisely for God's creation and uses recycled paper whenever possible.

About the author: For the last four years, Marvin and his wife, Sharisse and their children have been in his hometown of Norwich England. There he had his own counseling practice where he specializes in Marriage and Family therapy, also Anger and Stress Management. Marvin's practice catered to those of all religions but most of his cliental had no religion. Growing up an atheist himself for half his life and now a spiritual mined person gives him a unique worldview. He has a Masters Degree in Pastoral Counseling and has spoken/taught on various subjects all over the world. If you enjoy this book checkout his first book *Baguette Moments: Learning the Power of Entrustment.*

ILLUMINATION **ip** PUBLISHERS

www.ipibooks.com
6010 Pinecreek Ridge Court
Spring, Texas 77379-2513

Contents

Acknowledgements

I would like to thank everyone that God has put in my life to refine me to the person who I am, from those I befriended as a child (on the playground) to friends who have stuck by me for years. Without them, I would not have had the experiences to write this book. Some of my main influences in my later life have been my wife and kids, without whose love and patience I wouldn't be half the person I am today.

I want to thank Sharisse Lucas, Kim Romaine and Brandon Clayton for initially editing my work and making some sense of my babble!

For Appropriate Teen Reading:
Introduction, Chapters 1, 2, 6, 7, 8, 10, 11, 12, 13, 14, 15, 16, 17, 19, 20, 21, Appendix I

Introduction

Recently I was reminiscing about the '70s with my mother, and she spoke of me having a plastic Batman suit, a plastic mask and a black cotton cape that I wouldn't take off and that many a night I would even sleep in. To this day I can't remember the suit—although it probably fell off my body because I wore it out! What I do remember is watching *Batman* the TV show with my brother and getting so excited when the fight scenes would break out with "Boof," "Bam" and "Boom" as they hit the bad guys. My brother and I would get all ramped up, and after the show we would reenact it. However, no one wanted to be the Joker, the Penguin or, yuck, Cat Woman; we both wanted to be Batman and we fought over that privilege (with a "Bam" and a "Boom"!). From a young age we wanted to be the hero and rid the world of evil and pending doom. The first reading materials that I read voluntarily were comic books where I envisioned myself being Superman or Green Hornet or some other superhero. As I grew up, my first career choice was to be a police officer and bring justice to my hometown, but I failed the written test. Then I wanted to the join the army but failed the physical because of my asthma. My days of fighting evil were over, so I worked at a restaurant with my mum.

I've known my wife for twenty-five years, and she often shares childhood stories of her pretend play. My personal favorite is when she would role play in the mirror putting a white towel on her head imagining she had long flowing blond hair (but underneath was an afro!) and pretending to be her favorite movie star, Farrah Fawcett. My wife grew up poor and found solace from her circumstances by dressing up as a princess and other characters. Jumping forward years later to our wedding day, I remember it as if it were yesterday. She stood at the doorway of the sanctuary with her grandfather. She was radiant in her flowing white wedding dress, and as she walked down the aisle there were white flowers sprinkled on the floor. As she walked toward me, I could see her face and her nervous smile (I was nervous too) and as I looked closer, under the white veil I saw a tiara on her brow! The Princess adorned. What a moment; I will never forget it. She had come a long way from the white towel in the mirror. Even though we are in our forties now, I still want to protect her and be her superhero, but it's hard to find an XXL cape as you get older and fatter. (I now know how Mr. Incredible must have felt!)

These childhood dreams are timeless. In this generation my son plays out his heroism on his PlayStation and wants to defeat evil with his virtual cape in his bedroom. What a difference a generation can make, but the inherent desire is the same. Our daughter's first costume was a princess dress. I remember it was blue and covered with shiny sequins, with a plastic tiara. She paraded around in her mother's high heels (big shoes to fill!). In a recent move I had to clean out her room and saw in her drawer several tiaras. She's a teenager now, too old to wear tiaras, but she didn't throw them out—why? She's holding on to them because the dream is still there in her heart of living the life of a princess.

Some of the happiest memories for me were as a child. Even though I had a challenging childhood, it seems as an adult I have to fight to get back the innocence, peace and contentment that my childhood offered. I remember being out playing for hours, losing track of time and coming home exhausted by all the folly, but as the years went by, my childlikeness was wrung out of me by a dysfunctional upbringing and poor life choices. Many of us as adults are consumed with worry, stress and seriousness, causing physical, emotional and mental conditions that can kill us. As a therapist, I've seen the kind of damage stress and anxiety can do to a soul. Watching my mother recover from a stroke only served to reinforce this reality.

What happened? Where did our boyhood courage go? Where did that princess innocence and the search for the "happily ever after" love and chivalry go? I believe it's still accessible. You might be thinking that I am telling you to go to your mother's attic and grab your action figures or have a big-girl sleep over with a dress-up time. No, I'm talking about purging out childishness and living with childlike values that will give you a quality of life that few obtain. After spending nearly fifty years on this planet, I have been rejuvenated by embracing the power and tenderness of childlikeness, and I am excited to share my journey with you. I want to say to my mum, I'm still wearing my cape; it might be worn and tattered in places and it's a lot larger now to fit around my waist, but I do feel that I'm making a difference in my marriage, my family and the lives of those around me. In this day and age some would consider that heroic! In the chapters ahead we will take a holistic look at this concept of childlikeness through scientific, cognitive and spiritual lenses. It's time to tap into your inner superhero or princess. It's still there!

To Anna Baker,
My prayer is
that this book
will awaken the
childlikeness
in you

Part I

The Scientific Perspective
on Childlikeness

Chapter 1

Gaofen Dineng

Adults whom we call geniuses are those who somehow retain and build upon that childlike capacity throughout their lives.
—Dr. Peter Gray, Psychologist, www.independent.co.uk

I was in the public park by my house last summer listening to some music, having some "me time" between work and my kids coming home from school, when a group of public middle school kids took over the park jumping on swings and sliding down slides (more running up them), interrupting my time with their frolicking and loudness. Initially, I became annoyed, but I had to check myself and stop my "grumpy old man" attitude. I knew these kids; I went to the same middle school, and they came from working class homes as I did. From this very school it took me an hour to walk home (only ten minutes if I was in a hurry). I would rather do anything than go home, so on a warm summer afternoon in England (there aren't many), it was a no-brainer! Just like me, what were they going home to? An empty house, domestic unrest, constant disappointment or more structure. Recalling this, I unplugged my ears and took in the laughter and carefree spirit of the children. These kids walked together and had found a respite between school and home. For many of them this may have been the only time in their day to feel free and be a child. In this fleeting moment these kids had no parents, no teachers, no rules, no expectations, just pure unadulterated fun. My heart was full and their play reminded me of the good in my childhood. Children, keep on screaming, laughing and playing. Kids being kids, where did all that joy go?

Personal Freedom

As a child, playing outside was the "great escape" for me. My mother had four kids by the age of twenty-two. For years, my relationship with my father was strained and I found the streets to be a safer place. Even with my siblings, we couldn't do anything without arguing or physically fighting. This volatile environment pushed me out of the house. We could not afford toys and media that I could use to block out the dysfunction, so my solace was found out on the playground. People became my entertainment; when we were not playing football (soccer), doing nothing was fun. My desire to stay out was so great that some days it would be freezing or pouring down rain and I would leave the house in the morning and not come home until 9:00 at night. The playground molded me to be sharp-witted and creative, and the football and cycling to places kept me healthy.

This social confidence gave me the courage to get my first job at the age of ten at a local corner grocery store. Earning money made me feel empowered, and sometimes I was in charge of the store. When I was thirteen, I worked in a restaurant washing dishes, when I was fourteen I was making desserts and by fifteen I was working in the main kitchen directing professional chefs. Without any college education I went on to become a licensed investment broker and eventually became the top male rookie for a Fortune 500 company. People admired my drive, the people skills I had learned at a young age and my personal confidence. (Read about this empowering process in my first book, *Baguette Moments*.[1]) I was free not by intentional parenting but parental overwhelmedness. We hear the saying "I learned from the school of life" or "...the school of hard knocks." Those who normally say this are those who barely got through high school and yet became successful. Yes, I have lived both sides of the coin: today I sit here with a master's degree, an author and certified counselor, but when I reflect on almost fifty years of life, what truly defined me is what I learned on the playground.

The Power of Play

When kids play by themselves they understand fairness, social cues and negotiation. The playgrounds can be a brutal place where kids learn to play fair or no one will play with them. Play is by mutual agreement and all have the right to simply walk away. There were times when we had no ball and we kicked a stone around or created a game out of nothing; if not, we would amuse ourselves by making fun of each other. This verbal banter made me quick-witted. Yes, sometimes we got into fights because you protected your boundaries (we were too immature to talk it out) but there was a social order on the playground with not an adult in sight. Because of the lack of love at home and my immense insecurities, it didn't take much to start a fight. In most situations I could bully my way out of anything. Those who have been coddled don't have these learned boundaries; they have no emotional limits in relationships and wonder why they have low self-esteem and lack passion to fight. Today, parents are everywhere; in any dispute while having their "play date" the parent will step in and talk to the parent or the child. Others say nothing and don't go back there because that child didn't play nice. That's another opportunity lost to teach a child a valuable life lesson.

We also learned our physical limitations through play. As children we would take a moped through the woods with no helmet, jump from trees, and cycle too fast downhill. The bruises and cuts taught me that I wasn't invincible. Getting in fights and winning most and losing some taught me "you're not all that." Some kids today are "protected" by parental paranoia and walk through childhood with no consequences. They feel that mum will save them from everything, like when the bike breaks down in the rain and she runs out to pick them up or when college money is spent on an iPhone instead of food and they are bailed out nevertheless. You can see where this is going! The childhood years are crucial for learning to live a balanced life. Here's more proof:

> *Researchers have raised young monkeys and rats in ways such that they are allowed other types of social interactions but are deprived of play. When these animals are tested, in young adulthood, they are emotional cripples. When placed in a moderately frightening environment, they overreact with fear. They panic and freeze in a corner and never explore the environment and overcome the fear as a normal monkey or rat would. When placed with an unfamiliar peer, they may alternate between panic and inappropriate, ineffective aggression. They are incapable of making friends.*
>
> —Dr. Peter Gray

If you fast-forward thirty years, little Jimmy and little Cindy are no longer children but their characters have not developed as they should have. And they are sitting on my therapy couch having a meltdown as I listen to their plight of being overwhelmed with work, not meeting their spouses' needs and not being the best parent. When I analyze their situation, I conclude it's just life! Without minimizing their feelings, I must assert that if they had been conditioned from childhood to struggle, confront and reconcile, their reality would be a lot different as an adult. Developing princesses and superheroes falls to us, the parents. It can be painful at times and can bring a lot of angst in their little lives but it can save them in later life by making them less dependent on you the parent.

Learn from the Chinese!

As an up-and-coming superpower, China has a robust economy and an academic edge over us that must be admired. Some would even say that China owns America because of the debt bailout during the recent recession. Despite this academic and economic prowess, the Chinese government has great concern about the rearing of children and is taking acute action. Author Yong Zhao, who is an expert in Chinese schooling, discusses the term *gaofen dineng*, which means great at academic studying and nothing else. Some of China's children are anemic when it comes to interpersonal skills, creativity and discovering. Something the Chinese have relied on is stealing ideas from the West where creativity was sacrificed for the sole pursuit of an educated society. They succeeded but at what cost? In Beijing they have instituted mandatory play to foster "childlikeness" in children, according to Dr. Peter Gray:

> *Moreover, as revealed by a recent large-scale survey conducted by British and Chinese researchers, Chinese schoolchildren suffer from extraordinarily high levels of anxiety, depression and psychosomatic stress disorders, which appear to be linked to academic pressures and lack of play.*

Today, the pressures on school children in the USA are greater than ever. There are children as young as ten concerned about their college grades and stressed out of their childhood. They should be out with other kids playing in parks and arcades and scraping their knees. A typical ten-year-old is out playing and learning social skills. When I was a child, I would spend most of the time out of the house playing football and having a laugh with my friends.

Some parents might deceive themselves by believing that their children are driven and want to succeed, but many children go along because they don't want to upset their parents. A good test to see if the child wants to do the said activity is to say, "For a whole month there will be no playing piano or soccer" and see if they still want to do it. Will they practice without you prompting? Then you will know if it's their wish or your obsession. I know several adult clients who are in a profession that they really don't enjoy but their parents wanted it, so they went along to please them. For most children their desire is to please their parents, so unhealthy parental pressure can have serious emotional and developmental consequences.

In my practice, I have seen many a youth succumb to these emotional and cognitive problems. I am treating an eighteen-year-old whom I will call Ted, who for several months has been on antidepressants and spends all day in his room, as he has dropped out of college. The pressure of homework and the fear of failing became too much for him. Both parents are college educated and there is an unsaid expectation and pressure to do well at school. The young man feels that his parents look at him differently now since he started failing his courses, which led to his deep depression. When with his father, all they have spoken about and found common ground on was his college experience.

Some kids naturally pick their parents' hobbies because it's an opportunity to spend time with them and it's the only relatable element between them. I would give a caution to all parents to never put all your eggs in one basket. It could be sports or church, and if the child gets injured or doesn't want to go anymore, then the commonality is gone and in that child's mind so is your love. Many parents are concerned about the amount of media their children are consuming, but have you ever thought that you may have contributed to their withdrawal? The pressure of a one-dimensional life can be so great that one can see why kids escape to their PS4, Facebook and YouTube and shut themselves in their rooms. Some kids turn to food for comfort along with escaping indoors, which over time can have some health and mental issues.

Ted needs to get out of his bedroom, get around friends and be a child again. He should get a job to fill up his time and his mind and have some fun by creating a new hobby. His parents have had to reevaluate their relationship with their son and add another dimension in it other than education. I believe that Ted will go back to school on his own terms and his life will have other outlets, taking pressure off his academic performance.

In contrast to Ted, a child can be a great student but be self-centered, disrespectful and materialistic. There are some children who grow up being one-trick ponies, and if anyone asks them to do anything outside of studying they have a royal meltdown. When they leave home both parents still mother them. This unhealthy emphasis on one area of life sucks out the joy of childhood. Parental priorities of raising a child must be as follows: first and foremost is to develop a child's character to be a person who has an emotional, mental and spiritual aptitude. Second, children should learn to respect parents, get along with their siblings, relate to others and be a good friend, and help out domestically. Sometimes we are so caught up with a child not cleaning their room but allow them to be disrespectful to us. Wrong priorities! Cleaning up is about doing, but respect is about being. I can get my children to do things but is it their character? When your children are considerate and mindful of others and do things without being asked, you are well on your way. This takes years of nurturing and intentional parenting. When our kids are "being" then it's their character that's involved and they will carry on doing the right things into later years of their life.

Character building will help your child overcome adversity. Giving your child an easy ride at home is not developing them for real life, where they will hear "no" and have to multitask to survive. I would rather have my child go through his adolescent challenges under my roof than 200 miles away in college (and save me the trip). When they get to college they have to balance an ever-changing schedule, social life, peer pressure, washing clothes, budget and feeding themselves. That's a lot when they can't keep their room clean! Again, in those early years one must develop character and learn social etiquette through play.

Finding a Balance

Okay, Marvin. I'm going to have a child who will play all day with no responsibility and drop out of school! Looking at the data and my personal experience through my own narrative and my counseling, I would rather have a child who finds themselves through play and trial and error than a one-trick pony with no coping skills. As a parent we must give our children the freedom to work out conflict on the playground and as they get older let them find independence. Intentional parenting must be at the forefront of a child's development. Play and emotional responsibility in balance can open up a child to reach their full potential, something that as an adult Einstein found out.

Adult Play!

> *Adults whom we call geniuses are those who somehow retain and build upon that childlike capacity throughout their lives. Albert Einstein said his schooling almost destroyed his interest in mathematics and physics, but he recovered it when he left school. He referred to his innovative work as "combinatorial play."*
> —Dr. Peter Gray

Most parents would love their children to leave an impression on the world like Einstein did. But the schooling system almost pushed a genius to quit! Where would we be if Einstein were burnt out on academia? Albert Einstein was a prodigy but also was childlike at heart; he found the balance and didn't take his work too seriously. Let his life be a lesson that a combination of play and work will always bring the best out of an individual. This first chapter sets up the premise for the whole book as we look at the world through the eyes of a child again with a sense of wonder, excitement and creativity while still being responsible and considerate to others.

Chapter 2

The Pursuit
of
Childlike Happiness

An article came out on how to do ten simple things to make you happy based on several scientific studies. Please check out the website (https://blog.bufferapp.com/10-scientifically-proven-ways-to-make-yourself-happier). It shows neural scans while doing some of these activities and how the brain reacts to these principles. It's fascinating stuff.

Here are the top ten things to do to make us happier:

1. Exercise more
2. Sleep more
3. Move closer to work
4. Spend time with friends and family
5. Go outside
6. Help others
7. Practice smiling
8. Plan a trip
9. Meditate
10. Practice gratitude

After looking at this list, I noticed that the same activities that make adults happy also make kids happy (except for a shorter commute time). We complicate things as adults. Instead we should keep a childlike perspective and keep it simple. We are going to analyze several of these principles and see the correlation between one's happiness and having a childlike mindset.

Step One to Happiness According to Science:
BE ACTIVE AND EXERCISE

In a study cited in Shawn Achor's book, The Happiness Advantage, three groups of patients treated their depression with either medication, exercise, or a combination of the two. The results of this study really surprised me. Although all three groups experienced similar improvements in their happiness levels to begin with, the follow-up assessments proved to be radically different:

*The groups were then tested six months later to assess their relapse rate. Of those who had taken the medication alone, 38 percent had slipped back into depression. Those in the combination group were doing only slightly better, with a 31 percent relapse rate. **The biggest shock, though, came from the exercise group: Their relapse rate was only 9 percent!***
—Belle Beth Cooper, blog.bufferapp.com

As adults and children we should be active. My boy burns so many calories from his five-mile round trip to school and playing soccer every day he can't consume enough calories to sustain his active life. Unfortunately, this is not the norm for most kids as they confine themselves to their bedroom, their media cave. On the other hand, in our narcissistic society, it is sad when male teens feel the only acceptable body image is having a "six pack" and young girls are plummeting into depression over a pound of fat. Having two teens, I hear the conversation that happens with their peers and it is shocking how their appearance can dictate their whole worldview.

When I see an overweight child I often get angry at the parents because they are the ones that decide what their child should eat. The child has no money to purchase their own food. At an early age they get a taste and craving for unhealthy foods and this only continues when they get older.

As adults, we can choose careers where we are restricted to a desk and an hour commute in our cars, thus living a sedentary lifestyle. Some days our exercise is walking from the water cooler to our desk. By being active like children we feel alive as we produce endorphins that act as a natural antidepressant. Active kids are happy kids and active adults are happier too.

Step Two to Happiness According to Science: GET GOOD SLEEP

Over 82 million (40%) U.S. adults and teens suffer from some type of insomnia.... As they age, it only gets worse. 54% of people over age 55 report sleeplessness once or more a week. Sleep deprivation costs $45 billion a year in lost productivity, health-care bills, and expenses related to traffic accidents, rivaling the impact of depression...or stroke.

—BusinessWeek, 1/26/04

It seems as we get older, we get less sleep. The expression "sleep like a baby" is only for babies or for the childlike. Why is it that we get less sleep as we get older? Maybe it's the increased stress from the ever-growing responsibilities of life. Many of us could get eight hours a night but our consciousness won't let us. We have to medicate ourselves or drink a couple of glasses of wine to numb our consciousness to sleep. In Appendix I we will look at some solutions to get that babylike sleep back.

Step Four to Happiness According to Science: BE CLOSE TO FAMILY

Insights of [a] study on how men's social connections made a difference to their overall happiness: the men's relationships at age 47...predicted late-life adjustment better than any other variable, except defenses. Good sibling relationships seem especially powerful: 93 percent of the men who were thriving at age 65 had been close to a brother or sister when younger.

—Belle Beth Cooper

As my parents age, all I'm left with as immediate family are my siblings. I grew up in a family where reconciliation was not a staple. There's not a week that goes by when I don't lament over my relationship with my brother. We are only twenty months apart and when we were younger we did everything together, even dating the same girls! I started this book with a story of my brother and me reenacting Batman, but those days are so long ago. Do you have a parent or sibling or a loved one with whom you are in conflict? Send them a Christmas card or a birthday card and open up the dialog, because deep down they miss you too! In the following chapter we will explore how our upbringing affects our childlikeness.

Step Six to Happiness According to Science: HELP OTHERS

We scientists have found that doing a kindness produces the single most reliable momentary increase in well-being of any exercise we have tested.
—Martin Seligman, University of Pennsylvania professor

As parents it is an ongoing endeavor to get our kids to be conscious of others, helping them think about more than themselves and purging out the childishness while keeping childlikeness. No one likes a selfish person, and to be honest, no matter how good-looking you are, selfishness makes you ugly. Unfortunately, we are living in an increasingly self-absorbed society where people like Paris Hilton and Kim Kardashian are idolized and glorified by the media on reality TV, making it harder to say to my kids that that lifestyle is unfulfilling. It seems that fewer people are thinking of others and more are thinking about themselves.

On one vacation we went to Cancun, Mexico and I did not like how my kids were whining and complaining while experiencing our all-inclusive paradise. I decided to devote some time to visiting the poorer neighborhoods. My wife and I grew up in poorer communities so we were not fazed by being around folk like this, but the kids were reluctant. We went to the store and the kids picked out toys and candy and we got some food. The neighborhood I chose in which to give out these goods was on the outskirts of town where there was no running water or electricity and the dwellings were made of sheets of wood and corrugated steel. Going up to the shacks we saw that most had no doors and people were sleeping in hammocks (to get up off the floor because of the rats?). My daughter, who was six at the time, was afraid to go near the homes, but I insisted that she look at the way these people lived and what they had. One girl about her age had a doll that was filthy and missing a couple of limbs but she seemed to be really attached to it. The little girl was happy and oblivious of her poverty, as most children have no consciousness of their economic status and enjoy the simple things in life. When we showed her the dollar toys we had, she thought it was Christmas. These same toys would be lost in my kids' toy chest and thrown out eventually! The experience was great for all of us, and for a few days the whining and complaining died down.

I recently helped move a friend who is twenty-eight and single. When I arrived at his place, it was filthy. I was shocked that someone could live like this; no wonder he was single! I heard voices in his apartment; it was his little brother and his fifty-plus-year-old mother on her knees cleaning his filth. She had travelled seven hours to help him move. As we moved the first load in her SUV, she was seething mad and spoke about his previous moves and how she was the one called in to clean up his mess to keep his security deposit. I asked her if he cleaned up his bedroom when he was younger and she said, "No." Ah ha! Dysfunction is the gift that keeps on giving. Note to parents: it is easier to teach little Jimmy when he is eight rather than when he is twenty-eight! As long as we keep bailing out our kids, they will remain childish and not change. They will remain oblivious to their selfishness and how they hurt others, which is the opposite of being considerate and helping others.

Step Seven to Happiness According to Science: SMILE AND LAUGH

Smiling makes us feel good which also increases our attentional flexibility and our ability to think holistically. When this idea was tested by Johnson et al. (2010), the results showed that participants who smiled performed better on attentional tasks which required seeing the whole forest rather than just the trees.

—Belle Beth Cooper

Children are happy; they live for the moment and live out each day to the fullest. As we get older, we make things very complicated and that childlike perspective dissipates. In our workplaces it seems if you are not stressed you are not working! But if the findings of this scientific study are correct, having a light and joyous environment will increase productivity and create a better spirit in the workplace. To keep your childlikeness you need to be in a workplace that can be full of laughter but productive.

I called up my cable company because for six weeks of service I was charged $860.12. I was perplexed and quite angry about the overcharge. After I waited for twenty minutes, the customer rep got on the phone. He was so joyful and disarming, he alleviated my stress in a few seconds. I really felt he wanted to help me. As my anxiety subsided, I asked him how he could do this job where everyone calls and complains. He explained that in his small town this was the best job in that area. He had left Los Angeles and his career in the entertainment business to take care of his mother who was now recovering from cancer. His spirit came through the phone; his joy acted as a shield to negativity and was a valuable lesson for me. He is a caring man with a childlike heart in a challenging job. This man had his Superman cape on and was a hero in my eyes.

Step Eight to Happiness According to Science: PLAN A TRIP—HAVE SOMETHING TO LOOK FORWARD TO

A study...showed that...the effect of vacation anticipation boosted happiness for eight weeks.

—Belle Beth Cooper

Growing up poor and not having a car, travelling and taking vacations was challenging. We would take day trips by train to the beach. Once, my family and several other relatives went to a caravan site by a beach about twenty miles from my home. The thought of going on our first family vacation was exciting, and as the days approached, I got even more excited. Unfortunately the vacation wasn't the best. We had a swarm of black flies for several days and the family as usual started drinking and then started fighting.

One of my favorite things to do is to plan trips for the family:

the car rental, accommodation, flights, itinerary, tourist spots, and mapping out the mileage. I can spend hours getting the best deal. But the majority of the time it seems the anticipation and planning is more liberating than the experience. As I reflect, I can remember trips where something or someone has jeopardized our holiday experience: one of the kids being sick or complaining, leaving my wallet on the plane, having an accident in our rental car or being in a hotel where the suite next door was noisy. However, these unexpected interruptions did not stop us from planning the next trip with anticipation that this one would be the perfect vacation!

Young children have no concept of time, so if you tell them that in four months the family will go to Six Flags they will ask you every day until it happens. With my kids, their petitions got old quick, to the point that if they mentioned it one more time we were not going! Once I was planning a trip to Los Angeles and we got our hands on some cheap Disneyland tickets. This time we waited until two days before the date to tell our kids. We'd learned our lesson. Even in the wonderland of Disney, it was hot, the lines were long and my feet hurt, but the kids had a good time. I had more fun planning and watching them have a good time than from the trip itself.

Without planned trips or a vacation, life would be one dimensional and all we would be left seeing in front of us would be work and the mundane. It is good to have something to look forward to. I can see now this principle would help one's happiness.

Step Nine to Happiness According to Science:
MEDITATE

Meditate: think deeply or focus one's mind for a period of time, in silence...as a method of relaxation.
The Oxford Dictionary

When I was a kid, timeouts were not the discipline of choice in my house. As typical boys we would start at 8 a.m. and go until 9 p.m. Normally by 12 p.m. we were at critical mass and my mum had had enough. She would throw something at us or shout at us, and if she could catch us she would hit us to calm us down. Today parents have timeouts, naughty corners and quiet time. It was not until my twenties until I even considered an "Adult Time Out" through meditation and prayer. Even in my practice, I have seen so many people who were constantly on the go with kids, work and responsibilities. Their minds had no rest, especially if they were not sleeping well. For one of my clients, a condition of therapy was that for twenty minutes a day she had to stop and do nothing; if not I would not see her! I saw that she was a different person when she was centered; otherwise she couldn't hold a thought and wasted our time and her money. Please check out the neural scan in the bufferapp.com article that was taken before and after meditation; it's pretty amazing (I'm a believer).

> ## Step Ten to Happiness According to Science: BE GRATEFUL
>
> *The Journal of Happiness studies published a study that used letters of gratitude to test how being grateful can affect our levels of happiness:*
>
> *Participants included 219 men and women who wrote three letters of gratitude over a 3 week period.*
>
> *Results indicated that writing letters of gratitude increased participants' happiness and life satisfaction, while decreasing depressive symptoms.*
>
> —Belle Beth Cooper

Saying "please" and "thank you" was something my parents insisted on when I was young, but with today's growing entitlement generation, "please" and "thank you" are a rarity. Saying "thank you" seems so insignificant but it says so much. It says, "I see that you have denied yourself and served me." Thank you says that I don't take things for granted and I will treasure this or use it wisely. Young children do not earn money and have no way to pay back what they have been given until they are older; the sooner they realize this the more grateful they become.

As adults we spend so much time focusing on what we don't have rather than what we do have. We are so consumed by tomorrow; on developing our career, kids' college, buying a house and retirement, that we don't enjoy today. Remember that two thirds of this world lives on less than a dollar a day but when you look at the happiest countries, America is not ranked high among them considering what we have. Places like Costa Rica, Mexico and Panama are happier places (see the World Happiness Report 2013 at unsdsn.org). I've been to Mexico, and it's significantly poorer than the USA but the people do seem happier; it seems that the accumulation of wealth and of stuff doesn't mean happiness. If children are taught to be grateful it's a trait that they will take with them through life.

Chapter 3

Our Fatherless Society

63% of youth suicides are from fatherless homes — 5 times the average. (US Dept. of Health/Census)

90% of all homeless and runaway children are from fatherless homes — 32 times the average. (fclu.org)

85% of all children who show behavior disorders come from fatherless homes — 20 times the average. (Center for Disease Control)

80% of rapists with anger problems come from fatherless homes —14 times the average. (Justice & Behavior, Vol 14, p. 403–26)

71% of all high school dropouts come from fatherless homes — 9 times the average. (National Principals Association Report)

Daughters of single parents without a Father involved are 53% more likely to marry as teenagers, 711% more likely to have children as teenagers, 164% more likely to have a pre-marital birth and 92% more likely to get divorced themselves. Morse, Jennifer Roback, "Parents or Prisons," Policy Review, 2003

—unitedfatherssocal.org

71% of pregnant teenagers lack a father....

Fatherless boys and girls are: twice as likely to drop out of high school; twice as likely to end up in jail; four times more likely to need help for emotional or behavioral problems.

—US DHHS press release, Friday, March 26, 1999

2.5 million: Number of single fathers, up from 400,000 in 1970. Currently, among single parents living with their children, 18 percent are men.

—livescience.com

The Fatherless

The African-American community has been devastated by fatherless parenting. Seventy percent of African-American kids grow up without a father in their lives. The impact on this culture has been heart-breaking. Having an African-American father and being a victim of this systemic fallout is one of my reasons for writing this book; it's only by God's grace that I have avoided many of the cultural traps. Some people grew up with a mother and father but their fathers were disconnected and emotionally unavailable. Many dads, to their credit, provided physically for their family through working and bringing home the dough and being physically present at birthdays, parent-teacher meetings etc. However, when a father is not engaged with his children they become emotionally fatherless. Many dads leave the emotional stuff to their wives and might get involved when they are forced. Boys need their fathers to engage and show them how a man handles challenging situations without shutting down or needing anger management. Men bring up men. Dads bring the "why not" to life. They bring the rough-and-tumble play, the risk and the learning through the bruises of life. Many mums are consumed by the "what ifs" in life and are constantly looking out for hazards, not wanting their twenty-year-old baby to get hurt! More boys are influenced by their mothers and are sensitive and considerate but not risk-takers.

Our society becomes feminized by the mums because they are the ones who are more involved in school activities and their child's life. For eight years I was the director of an elementary camp. The kids were there for five days, and every year I had several mothers volunteering to be camp helpers, but getting the dads to help was like pulling teeth. In the girls' cabins I had two or three mums. For the boys I had maybe one dad and sometimes just two interns in their twenties to help. Many a time while playing dodge ball, a girl would get accidently hit in the face and start crying. A couple of mothers would pull me aside and petition to stop playing that activity because it was too rough for their princess. Many school authorities succumb to this constant pressure and as a result we have a no pain/no risk environment for our kids. This can have a profound effect on one's social and emotional development. This again is what we should have learned on the playground, which I spoke about in chapter one.

Without pain or risk, there will be no future superheroes; our capes will be used for tablecloths at the next princess tea party! Mums don't do it. Let boys be boys!

Most fathers who read this will feel overwhelmed by the emotional and physical chasm that has developed between them and their wife and kids. Seek help from a friend, a counselor or a church and come up with a plan of redemption. Women are forgiving when they believe that you are doing something to change. Kids will push back initially (they are hurt) but deep down they want that paternal love. Fathers, be a hero and be there physically and emotionally for your children.

Part II

Emotional and Cognitive Aspects of Childlikeness

Chapter 4

Searching for Dad

Although one side of my childhood was empowering, I lacked emotional guidance and a father figure. Here is a snapshot of my desperation for a mentor: Bob was twenty-five years older than I. We met in Belgium (I was there because I didn't want to go home) and we became friends. He was flashy, funny and seemed to have his life together. He had a BMW and wanted to travel. I was burned out from working in a pub seventy to eighty hours a week and it seemed like a good escape. I didn't want to go back to England and be a failure; I was running away from my domestic dysfunction. Bob was friendly at first but after becoming dependent on him for my wellbeing, he exploited me, putting me in debt while being emotional and mentally abusive.

Over the months, I felt more trapped and was involved in different criminal activities. It reached a crisis point when we were involved in a high-speed chase through Amsterdam with the Dutch police. This was adult play now! This was no longer kids pushing each other on the playground. How was I going to deal with this? It was time to take my ball and go back on the streets. I would rather be homeless than put up with this abuse. The survival skills I developed from the playground came in handy. I went out and begged for loose change and after a few hours I would have enough for food. I did this for a few days. During this time I used my relationship skills (again, developed on the playground) to meet a total stranger, Michael. Over the next couple of days we spoke about my situation and he asked me to stay at his place. He gave up his bed and slept on the floor! I was homeless but safe. He even gave me money to get home. In my time of need, being a rounded social person helped me to connect with people and build relationships. To this day, I am indebted to Michael. Over the years I have done a lot of research to find him by doing Internet searches and calling overseas, but I have not found him. The Michaels in this world give me hope in mankind. What an unsung hero!

My episode with Bob opened my eyes to evil, teaching me to be wise in my friendships and that fun and flashy can be dangerous. Through these experiences, I witnessed extremes of exploitation and benevolence. I learned a valuable lesson, painful but priceless. Many like me have to learn the hard way. Hopefully we come out with only a few bumps and bruises and nothing too damaging. I met Bob in an attempt to fill the void of a missing father presence; I was haphazardly drifting through life looking for a moral and masculine compass. Desperate for mentorship in my life, I needed guidance, and left to myself, I was now vulnerable and open for being exploited. I wish my father had been one who showed me how to navigate through tough relationships and helped me distinguish between safe and unsafe ones. That way, I might have seen someone like Bob coming a mile away. As fathers, we must do our part to show our children what a trustworthy man looks like and not leave them to roll the dice for role models on the street in the form of their peers, rappers or movie stars. With intentional parenting you can let your child experience toxic people in small doses so the sting of that interaction will make them aware that people like this are out there and will train them not to be naïve.

Chapter 5

A Homeless Child

In the situation with Bob, the real crime was that I would rather be homeless than go or call home for help! I was fortunate to have an angel to scoop me off the streets so I did not have to suffer abuse again. Many do not have that good fortune. In their desperation they go from one abusive relationship to another because they have no home or safe place to go to. I have clients who are strippers and prostitutes, and the common theme is that they have poor relations with their parents. So the exploitation continues. They have lost their tiaras running from one abuse to another. This breaks my heart!

Many teens make it hard for their parents to tolerate their disrespectful and harmful behavior. Many of their parents have other children and they are concerned with the influence of the teen on their siblings. As parents we cannot approve of drug use, alcohol abuse and rebellion against house rules. After months of this, if the child is old enough, they have to make a choice to stay and change or go and live their life. Some kids act out because of a lack of attention; their bad behavior makes the parents focus on them. Many parents make a huge mistake: they can't differentiate between love and tolerating sin. Their love is based on the child's behavior, which makes their love conditional. The child then feels that their parents hate them because of their actions. Some may leave the home feeling unloved and now are at the mercy of the streets. The odds are that they will find many Bobs and Bobettes out there! They have nowhere to go when life turns sour. Many kids are not that rebellious but they don't feel any love at home. Due to this conditional type of love they might become reluctant to seek advice or come home when they are in trouble.

Love Is Always Your Plan B

If your child leaves home knowing that they are loved and will always be welcomed back home, then life does not become a one-way street. If they have a safe place to come back to, they are not at the mercy of the street vultures. If they do fall prey to them, they don't have to stay out there. They can come home and cut the abuse off quickly, which limits the hurt and lets them step away from the situation to gain clarity. How many people feel stuck in an abusive relationship or marriage? If only they could go somewhere with the kids just for a few days. Having a place to regroup and reevaluate is priceless. We all need a place where we won't be judged but loved and empowered for the next chapter of our life. If we all had a home or safe place, we would not have the social dependences we see today on alcohol, drugs and self-harming, or the need for intensive therapy. There are millions of adult "children" out there who feel emotionally homeless. All they want to do is to go HOME to a loving, safe place!

What does a loving home look like? Here's the popular Prodigal Son story:

> "There was a man who had two sons. The younger one said to his father, 'Father, give me my share of the estate.' So he divided his property between them.
>
> "Not long after that, the younger son got together all he had, set off for a distant country and there squandered his wealth in wild living. After he had spent everything, there was a severe famine in that whole country, and he began to be in need. So he went and hired himself out to a citizen of that country, who sent him to his fields to feed pigs. He longed to fill his stomach with the pods that the pigs were eating, but no one gave him anything.
>
> "When he came to his senses, he said, 'How many of my father's hired men have food to spare, and here I am starving to death! I will set out and go back to my father and say to him: Father, I have sinned against heaven and against you. I am no longer worthy to be called your son; make me like one of your hired men.' So he got up and went to his father.
>
> "But while he was still a long way off, his father saw him and was filled with compassion for him; he ran to his son, threw his

arms around him and kissed him.

"*The son said to him, 'Father, I have sinned against heaven and against you. I am no longer worthy to be called your son.'*

"*But the father said to his servants, 'Quick! Bring the best robe and put it on him. Put a ring on his finger and sandals on his feet. Bring the fattened calf and kill it. Let's have a feast and celebrate. For this son of mine was dead and is alive again; he was lost and is found.' So they began to celebrate.*

"*Meanwhile, the older son was in the field. When he came near the house, he heard music and dancing. So he called one of the servants and asked him what was going on. 'Your brother has come,' he replied, 'and your father has killed the fattened calf because he has him back safe and sound.'*

"*The older brother became angry and refused to go in. So his father went out and pleaded with him. But he answered his father, 'Look! All these years I've been slaving for you and never disobeyed your orders. Yet you never gave me even a young goat so I could celebrate with my friends. But when this son of yours who has squandered your property with prostitutes comes home, you kill the fattened calf for him!'*

"'*My son,' the father said, 'you are always with me, and everything I have is yours. But we had to celebrate and be glad, because this brother of yours was dead and is alive again; he was lost and is found.'*" [2]

Run out to him and have a celebration? Really! Everything in my being would want him to walk up to the door and knock ten times, and then when I decided to open the door I'd say, "What are you doing here?" or "I knew you would come back, groveling!" Then I would leave him in the doghouse for a while until I made him feel how much he'd hurt me. The last thing would be a party! This young son showed himself the epitome of selfishness by asking for his inheritance from his father. This was almost saying, "I wish you were dead and I want my money now." Taking this money out of the family could jeopardize the whole farm and the workers could lose their jobs. He just wanted to have fun and leave his oppressive home life because he had to do his part pitching in with the chores around the farm.

I have learned that there's no point in beating a dog that has already beaten itself, and this boy was pulverized by his own poor choices and his own guilt. I know what it means to swallow one's pride and come home with one's tail between their legs. The prodigal son needed love, not judgment. When the son left, the father put no conditions on his returning, just left the front door open to love. Just imagine if the son had had nowhere to go. What would have happened to him and what might he have become? Instead, a father had a son who left selfish, ungrateful, arrogant and self-centered but returned humble, appreciative and willing to do whatever to help around the farm.

Some of us are delaying the process of refinement. Our prodigal child is destroying the sanity in our homes. Let them go with love! They are out of their senses and a real dose of life might knock some sense into them. Bailing them out of every hardship will keep them from appreciating things and they will continue to look to be rescued from basic life situations. Stop it, cut the umbilical cord, let them go and let them mature. It's painful, but they will live. In my practice I see more and more people in their forties with few or no coping skills, but they have their caring mum! Your job is to know when to let go; if you hold on too long it will only further fuel their rebellion and they might be out there longer. Let them go; they will come back different.

Prodigalize Our Homes

In this story we have a loving dad (yes, dads can be loving) with a prodigal son. Sometimes no matter what we do, their nature is greater than our nurture. One must have deliberate parenting when helping to develop a child's character. If they are selfish, talk about sharing and being considerate. Over and over again the child should be reminded and shown his selfish ways (choose your moments), but also greatly encourage the child when he shows glimmers of selflessness. Their selfishness will hurt people. One Mother's Day my son, who was about fourteen at the time, was reminded about a week before about the day coming up. He said that he was going to get something, and I had decided that I wasn't going to remind him again or take him out and do all the legwork that I had even done in previous years. This year he was on his own; he could cycle to the local store and he had the money. I didn't say anything else. Mother's Day morning came and my daughter had a handmade card and a piece of jewelry she picked out.

My son had nothing! Let me take that back: a bunch of excuses and nothing! My wife loves Mother's Day and birthdays and was deeply hurt to the point of tears. My son was shocked by her pain and he saw for the first time how his selfishness truly hurt others. He started crying! What a transformation from an excuse-making, flippant teen to a sobbing and convicted child. A painful but priceless lesson. If I had bailed him out, he would not have learned. My son is now eager to give, even making breakfast for his mum on these special days.

The Fear Factor

The loving father let his son experience his prodigalism first hand to learn a valuable life lesson. I see many children today who are so full of dread without leaving the house. They are paralyzed by their parents' paranoia! Ever since I can remember, if anyone in our family mentions our time in North London during the 1970s, my mum always brings up the mass murderer of Muswell Hill! This man would kidnap men and boys, torture and abuse them, then kill them and bury them in the ground of his basement. We only lived a couple of blocks away from his house, which was close to the school that we would walk to every day. When my mother talks about this, her intensity and dread resurfaces as if we still lived there today, but it was forty-plus years ago and is now 100 miles away. After doing further research for this book, I looked at our timeline living in Muswell Hill and the murderer's: we lived there from 1970 to 1971 and the murders happened between 1974 and 1978, so we were not even there during the times of the murders! For years I thought I was an arm's reach away from being abducted, sexually abused and buried in a basement. Knowing now that it wasn't true, I feel that I've wasted a lot of emotional energy on a myth for forty years of my life. I could have brought this gruesome story into my children's lives and passed on this paranoia. All this to say, be careful not to heap your own fears (real or not) on your child. Let them live out their own realities and help them process them in a rational manner.

The USA has become a place of fear: ISIS coming to America, and the Ebola virus could be here on the next plane to infect us! Did you know that during the flu season of 2003–04 there were 48,614 deaths in the USA (pediatrics.about.com)? Remember the bird flu pandemic of 2009, H1N1, with people wearing surgical masks, hand sanitizer in every public place, then millions of vaccinations ordered by congress? When the dust settled this virus had claimed between 8,870 and 18,300 lives in the USA (pediatrics.about.com). Any life lost under unexpected circumstances is painful, and I'm not minimizing this, but we have to put our fears into context. We should be more concerned about being seriously harmed by driving our car or the common flu, but the media doesn't cover that! Another example of this is that if we lived a hundred years ago, with no global communication media, unless we saw 9/11 happen or heard about it by word of mouth, we would never know and would live a life oblivious of it, in which case we wouldn't be paranoid when we saw a Muslim at an airport.

I worked at a health club on the West Side of Cleveland. There was a coworker who was from a small town in central Ohio. One day in the staff room a conversation started up about dating other races and this young lady of about twenty stated that "she would never date a black man!" I was shocked; I asked her if she'd had bad experiences with black folk. She said, "No," then she went on to explain that ever since she was a little girl her parents told her not to date black people. Wow, the power of parental paranoia! Her parents had conditioned her to embrace their fears and prejudice and had not given her a chance to form her own opinions by her own experiences. The same brainwashing can happen with relatives, church members, people in authority such as police or politicians, and neighbors. Kids overhear their venom and take on their prejudice. I want to let kids be kids and let them learn some lessons through their own experiences, not ours. It's hard to be a superhero when you are afraid to come out of the house, and it's hard being a paranoid princess in search of love but afraid of men.

Chapter 6

Emotional Childishness

Although Einstein's philosophy is true in regard to keeping a childlike spirit as you grow up, we can't be immature in our outlook on life and thus fail to take care of our responsibilities. As we get older, we become more aware of others, especially when we are in a serious relationship or have a family. Men have a problem with this transition. Many do well as a single but get overwhelmed by life's ever-increasing pressures and react with fright, flight or fight to deal with this, all of which are wrong. They act childishly by getting defensive, deflecting, running to mum, going out to the clubs, avoidance or turning to a substance such as alcohol. None of these reactions deal with what's happening at home. When we were single we could go to our room and shut out the world. Facing our fears and responsibilities is the only way to purge out our childishness.

The playground doesn't prepare you for the emotional playground of relationships. Women do better at this than men do. They are more emotionally astute and that's refined by their need for others and community. Many men are happy to sit in their man cave blocking out responsibility and the emotional complexities of life. My father didn't teach me how to be a gentleman. The "man" part is easy but the "gentle" part is challenging. So, getting into a long-term relationship was challenging for me; I wanted the sex without the drama. The problem is that as one gets more involved there's more at stake and the emotions build. What starts off as a fun relationship is now heavy and emotional. This always became too much for me; I had to go! I was childishly playing with people's emotions and hurting them deeply. Once at a seminar the speaker said that a person can heal quicker from a punch in the face than a deep emotional scar. As I've grown older I believe this to be true, and to my regret I believe that some of those women are less trusting and loving because of my treatment of them. I was an emotional wrecking ball and even today I lament over my actions.

How many people today are oblivious of their words and actions that lead to deep emotional contusions? In the playground I could punch my way out of anything, but in adult life I resorted to mental and emotional games. I went from a physical bully on the playground to an emotional bully in relationships. My dad knocked out of me stealing and disrespecting my mum, and I wish he'd knocked into me emotional awareness. My fatherless and homeless upbringing welled up in me a deep insecurity and hurt. Hurt people hurt people! I wasn't taking care of myself, so how could I have a relationship? I wasn't happy and childlike; I was a manipulator. I was playing with people's minds and hearts. I wanted to play the relationship game without the emotional responsibility.

In any close relationship you are going to get on each other's nerves and fall out sometimes. When these times occur it is paramount that reconciliation take place in order for the love and trust to continue to be. How we deal with conflict will dictate what kind of friend we are. When we respect each other we will be mindful of each other's feelings and conscious of what damage our words can do.

What Is Emotional Childishness?

Here are the top ten childish strategies used to not take responsibility for one's actions and words:

1. Losing one's temper or getting physical so the uncomfortable conversation will stop

2. Getting defensive and arguing using words like "I feel attacked" or "You're judging me"

3. Going into a sulk and looking for reassurance

4. Avoidance and hoping it will pass over (staying too "busy" to deal with it)

5. Turning the tables and bringing up the other person's past wrongs (Justifying bad behavior with bad behavior never works.)

6. Saying "sorry" but it's not heartfelt (then arguing, "I said I'm sorry, so it's over!")

7. Shedding crocodile tears and hoping that people will feel sorry for one

8. Focusing on the ten percent of the conversation that wasn't totally true and not the ninety percent that was right

9. Blaming one's upbringing or life circumstances for the failure to change

10. Minimizing the situation and stating that the other person is overreacting

None of these will bring closure, and the individual will not face their shortcomings and change. They will remain a childish child. Over the years I have used several of these strategies but they didn't bring about change.

Other childish traits that communicate selfishness are: when your yes is no, disrespecting people including parents, gossiping about others, being ungrateful, quitting too easily, blaming others for your life, expecting others to bail you out, getting in debt instead of saving up to pay for things, living in extremes, looking for shortcuts or a quick buck, and avoiding responsibility. All these will stop you from growing emotionally. Our emotional shortfalls can become magnified when we embark upon a long-term relationship.

Chapter 7

Frog Avoidance
(Staying a Princess)

In the Disney movie, we see the princess kiss the frog and he turns into a prince. But in real life no matter how much affection you give that toad, he is going to remain a toad! Unless your princess outfit comes with a magic wand, nothing is going to change him. And Hollywood doesn't help; we fantasize over movie stars, soap stars or famous entertainers and use that as a guide for love, but no one knows what's really going on behind closed doors. How many times have we been shocked to hear that famous people's relationships like Mariah Carey's or Beyoncé's are in trouble? But "they looked so happy!" We can base love on what we perceive it to be. Love is not just based on two people looking good on the red carpet "smiling" for the world. We somehow believe that with all their fame, money, looks and fitness, they will live happily ever after, and we are truly shocked when it doesn't happen. We live in a superficial world and can tend to care more about the physical without looking at what truly makes a relationship work. When we also add up our parents' relationship, what our friends are telling us and what we see through the media, we can get ourselves in trouble. There are few examples of functional relationships. We can hold on to our fantasy love and its accompanying philosophy, which will only bring heartache and disappointment. In my experience, there are few things in life that can impose more pain than a bad long-term relationship.

Many in their adolescence are eager to leave home because of real or perceived turmoil. Once someone promises them love and shelter on their lily pad, they are gone! Young women are so in love with the prospect of love that a young lad can come on his horse to save them from their "wicked stepparents" (their real parents). In their mind they are saved, but they overlook the character flaws of their so-called prince. They and their "prince" have something in common: they are both victims and find a bond in that; it's them against the world and their fledgling love will prevail! But what is that bubbling sound? Yes, under the veneer of love is dysfunctional slime from the frog pit that is ready to ooze out.

As a young man, I took advantage of naïve, unloved princesses looking for comfort from their family woes. My playground social skills made me sharp enough to chat up anyone. I enjoyed exploiting the innocent; it was fun. Most princesses in their desperation for love and affection run into frogs like I was. They were enamored by my carefree attitude and spontaneity, but just below the fun there was pain and lostness. Couples like that are two lost souls trying to find solace in each other. If someone would put the dysfunction facts on the table they wouldn't walk away from each other, they would run! But they hold on to their toad and as the relationship gets serious the frog slime (the upbringing dysfunction) starts to bubble up. For me, after the thrill of the chase and having got what I wanted, I would get bored and start treating the woman badly, like an alley cat playing with a cute mouse before the kill. After a few months of being in such a relationship, the once-naïve princess won't recognize herself, and her insecurities will have brought about an intense jealousy, paranoia, mistrust, and in some even violence and rage. The childlike joy is sucked out. Her tiara is lost in the craziness and mistrust.

The Vortex of Love and Dysfunction

This is a song that describes the extreme feelings that can come from love and dysfunction. Sadly, most women come out of their romances hardened and more untrusting of men.

You got a black heart.
Daddy, I've fallen for a monster.
Somehow he's scaring me to death,
Oh, yes he is!
He's big and he's bad.
I love him like mad.

Mamma, he's the best I ever had.
Daddy, I've fallen for a monster.
—Stooshe, "Black Heart" [3]

In the song, it sounds like this woman knows she made a mistake and is reaching out to her daddy like a little child. It's as if her childlikeness is screaming out for light and parental guidance. I have a daughter, and she will always be my little princess and I will be her daddy. It would be a tragedy to have my precious caught up in something like this. It would break my heart!

Reading the lyrics, it is sad when someone says a relationship like this is the best they ever had. In this vortex, she keeps on telling herself and others she loves him, but deep down she knows he has a black heart and has taken her to some dark places. When a princess is caught in the vortex of a dysfunctional relationship, it will only end up with her feeling ashamed of herself. To emphasize this point, a famous football player was shown in a hotel video knocking out his fiancée in an elevator and then a few weeks later she married the man! His rage was so intense that he could have killed her. Looking at the video, he didn't stop the elevator and get immediate help; he tried to save face and kept the doors closed, hoping that she would come around. He was not shocked by his rage. In my business, I know that abuse like this doesn't just happen; the early signs start with profanity, then fits of rage, then punching walls or throwing things, then raging at the woman, then grabbing her, then pushing her and before she knows it he's slapping or punching her.

No princess should be with a monster. My precious princesses, monsters don't have to beat you up to earn that title; they can oppress you by playing mind games, which is emotional abuse, making you feel like a street urchin and not like royalty. Once a bubbly princess, you become a shell of your former self. In your desperation for love and not wanting to say to your parents, "You were right!" you hold out in hope that one day he will give you the love you long for and will truly change. Maybe moving in with him, he will be more attentive— and then you're pregnant. The deception continues: you think surely having a child together he will get serious and responsible. But the reality is that as the responsibility grows he withdraws even more, and then you become more exasperated, thinking that degrading him with harsh words will show him how hurt you are and that the urgency of your situation will get him to change, but he doesn't. You feel trapped and alone. What went wrong? All you wanted was to be loved. Many women like this end up in therapy. Warning: One bad relationship can bring you to this point, and this traumatic experience can have a profound effect on future relationships and your propensity to love.

Castle Walls

The battle is won or lost in the vetting process. Whom you choose will dictate a large part of your life and how you live it. As you can see, a relationship can get away from you quickly and you can be stuck there alone with two screaming kids. How can we make your palace frogproof and protect your childlikeness? Remember, you are a princess, and wearing that tiara means you are royalty. It's time to restore your integrity and self-esteem and get that prince you deserve. You should walk like a princess, talk like a princess (no profanity or gossip), dress like a princess (cover yourself up), and don't associate with male peasants. Save yourself for a prince. I say again: Don't give yourself to a pauper, but save yourself for someone who deserves you. Men love a challenge and they will change their ways to get the prize. Hopefully through this endeavor they will fall in love with you and not be driven by their carnal lust.

Given my story, how did I go from being a cheating monster to a prince? My girlfriend at the time put her tiara back on. We broke up and she made it clear that my behavior had to radically change (I'll share my transformation story later), and she was serious. I had a choice to walk away or stay and change. We went on to get married and I've been faithful for twenty-three years. Healthy princesses set boundaries because they are royalty, and if their prince loves and cares for them he will abide by them. If not, send him to the pigs; he's not your prince. Don't compromise!

Chapter 8

Cowards in Capes

In the movie Superman, it was hard to watch when Lex Luther tricked Superman and put a chain hung with kryptonite around his neck. It was so sad to see Superman wearing his cape but so weak and vulnerable. We have a lot of men today masquerading in capes but they are cowards. If you are making adult choices you need to take on adult responsibility. If you are going to date someone, make sure you can look after yourself first and don't bring others into your madness. Having sex? Make sure you are man enough for the physical and emotional consequences. Society is being destroyed by men who are not committed to their partners and to raising their children. The stats on fatherlessness are overwhelming, and the multigenerational dysfunction it causes is staggering.

Most men think sex has no consequence, and Hollywood glorifies the idea that they can go through life having as many random partners as they want. So many people say it's just a casual relationship (friends with benefits), but one of the partners normally falls in love over time. When this happens, that person gets serious and wants more. They want the other person to commit, so they start to be controlling and obsessive. I was in such a relationship in my early twenties. She was a nice person, very conservative and wouldn't hurt anyone. Over time, I used her for her money, drove her new car while she took the bus to work, messed around with other women and played mind games. One day, the games and lies caught up with me, so I wasn't surprised when she snapped and came at me with a knife. I had to hold her down for an hour until she calmed down. All I was looking for was a little fun with no strings, and here I was stopping someone who wanted to kill me! Her only fault was that she fell in love with a pig; my madness did the rest. I was a pig, a frog, a monster, and I deserved nobody's love. She was not the only woman I played games with; I even did it to my wife while we were dating. My actions made many women more jaded. Sadly, even if their prince finally came along, they were damaged by my shenanigans and unable to trust men again. Eventually, I came to the end of my self, which I will talk about later in the book. The bottom line is, if you are going to wear the cape of manhood, wear it with pride and be ready to take on the emotional responsibility of a wife and family. This is my superhero and he deserves a cape. Superheroes protect their loved ones (like Superman protects Lois Lane). They are faithful and loyal in marriage to the end.

Chapter 9

I've Married a Frog!

Many married women show up at my office at their wits' end. After months of nagging, screaming, threats of leaving and then when they have no more words left adopting the silent treatment, still nothing has worked for them. At this point the wives are taking full responsibility for the kids and running the house; their husband is there physically but emotionally checked out—the lights are on but no one is home. Many women talk about the early years before the kids and responsibilities when their husband seemed to be available and more engaged. Most women forget that their husband could barely look after himself when he was single. They could handle that early level of relationship but in some cases the woman wants to accelerate things because she has found "the one." Now in their thirties she wants kids and/or fulfillment of her idyllic fantasy of what a marriage and family life should look like, complete with an elaborate wedding, new cars, buying a house, etc.

In your defense you say that he agreed to all of it, but the truth is, he didn't want to put up with the tantrums or silent treatment or being in the doghouse for days if you didn't get your way. The reality is that your husband has the emotional aptitude of a frog. Sadly, you may have piled more materialism and responsibility of kids on him in the space of a couple of years and now you are frustrated and wondering why he's not there. He is overwhelmed and has gone back to his emotional lily pad of escaping with TV, hobbies, working all hours, video games, alcohol, pot smoking or even extramarital affairs. But, my frustrated princess, there is hope! Realizing this dynamic is fifty percent of the problem, and to get him back on dry land, he needs achievable goals to find his courage and feel like he is doing something right for once. Encouraging the good you see will help him to feel like an empowered man and not like a beaten-down toad. With patience and love, your frog will become a prince. Here's a story of a marriage in desperate need of getting back the childlikeness:

My heart began to sink and my eyes filled with tears as I read sentences like:

"Hello gorgeous, how's my darling, sexy, charming, romantic, thoughtful, loving man doing?"

"I miss you so much I feel like I'm going to go crazy!"

"I feel like something wonderful is getting ready to happen in your life!"

All I could think was, Who is this girl?

Reading her letters, I was overcome by feelings of jealousy. She was sexy, fun, romantic and totally in love with my man! Some letters had hand-drawn images and others were sealed with a kiss, literally—with pink lipstick that looked as if it were just kissed yesterday.

I felt as if I were reading the letters of my husband's mistress, yet the truth was, it wasn't his mistress; these letters were from me, written as a twenty-something-year-old girl. I felt so many emotions, but most of all shame because that girl was long gone and in her place was a stressed out, anxious 40-year-old mother of two.

I no longer made Dave feel wanted, let alone desirable; but more like a roommate or friend. Reading the letters, I saw the loss of my girl, the one he fell in love with and married. Traci Shafer was encouraging, always laughing, dancing, singing and saw beauty in everything around her. Traci Bild, well...let's just say she had a lot on her plate.

In a strange way, I felt sorry for Dave. With my growing business, two kids and a home to manage, I simply didn't have the time or energy for him anymore. Closing the box, I tucked the letters back where I found them. I thought to myself, You've changed.

For days I thought about those letters. The passion and

emotion in them was intoxicating and I was tired of being tired. I wanted what my twenty-something year old girl had. *More importantly, I wanted what she and my husband had together, so I set out to find her.*

The first thing I did was make an effort to have more fun. When cleaning, I played blasting music, I traded the treadmill for kick boxing and the park bench for the swing next to my kids.

*Next, I started bringing fun into my marriage. From disco dancing in the kitchen...***to taking road trips together,*** our relationship returned to its roots with fun front and center. Slowly, the woman Dave married returned. The truth was she was there all along—she was just buried in responsibility.*

Being a woman today isn't easy; there's always going to be more to do than hours in the day. What I learned from this experience is the importance of prioritizing the things that matter most and having Dave at the bottom of that list wasn't going to work. I pushed him to the top and our family is better off for it. Here are a few more things I did that had lasting effects on our relationship. I encourage you to give them a try:

...

Make it fun! Make a vow: No dinner and a movie dates! When dating, odds are you and your husband did things that were fun. Try new and interesting things like playing racquetball or going bowling, taking a cooking class together or hitting a theme park and riding roller coasters! Does this take work? Yes, but it's worth the effort.

Create new habits.... The question to ask is, "Is my relationship worth it?" Compliment your man daily, give him a solid 20 minutes of your time every day, plan weekly date nights and have some good old-fashioned fun.

It's so easy to be apathetic and lament, "Why is this up to me, he doesn't do any of these things!" Could it be that your partner; is so disconnected he doesn't even think it's possible to reconnect again?...

In marriage, the odds are against us. We must be willing to roll up our sleeves and put in some work. This also means letting go of all ego or concerns over who's pulling the weight. I was no longer the girl my husband married, but I realized it before it was too late because he was too kind to tell me. It terrifies me to think how different my life and that of my children might have been if I had ignored the warning signs and not put my marriage on the list.

—Traci Bild, "The Day I Realized I Was No Longer the Woman My Husband Wanted"[4]

Well put, Traci! She found her tiara in a box full of old love letters. There is always hope, as long as there's childlikeness in your heart. This story epitomizes the power of unleashing the child in you; it can transform your relationship. This marriage had gotten boring and predictable, bogged down with life's "adultness" and in need of an injection of childlikeness. But what about a relationship that has gone down a worse path than this? Later in the book we will look at how to overcome abuse and deep emotional hurt with the power of childlikeness.

Chapter 10

Humility of a Child

The seeker after truth should be humbler than the dust. The world crushes the dust under its feet, but the seeker after truth should so humble himself that even the dust could crush him. Only then, and not till then, will he have a glimpse of truth.
—Gandhi, *The Story of My Experiments with Truth*[5]

When we think of learning, we automatically think of school or university. In life there is a difference between knowledge and life truths. We all gain knowledge, but there are very few who pursue life truths. Our educational system fills us up with knowledge that will help us get the career we desire. I've come across some brilliant people whom life's truths seem to have eluded. Many who excel in academia have a false sense of themselves. Pride eventually kicks in because society says you are educated and you are fully equipped for life. I have attended several colleges and universities, and many of these institutions have a built-in paranoia, causing them to go to great lengths to keep "their" truth and their sociopolitical views. They are frightened that students will exercise their free will and purchase a book that is not on the list of recommended reading material and is written from a different point of view. Some professors only have students read their published books or those of other professors within the same institution. It is scary to see how the masses unconsciously are corralled into a certain worldview. After several years of college education, my relationships and overall life saw little benefit. No one on their deathbed says, "I wish I had worked more" or "...got more education." It's in your last hours that life's truths catch up with you. We can look at some major academic minds (Nietzsche, Kofman, Gorz and Godel) who were tormented by their own knowledge and views that eventually led to their suicide. We can be full of secular learning but still feel so empty and lost inside.

Pride has many shades: we take pride in our academic achievements, the people we know, the way we're brought up, the places we have visited, what our kids are doing and things we buy and have. When Sharisse and I got married, we lived in debt and painted a materialistic picture that came across as if we had it all together. Over the years we lived this façade and ran up $40,000 of credit card debt. Too prideful to have an old car or secondhand furniture, it took us ten years to pay that off. We learned a hard lesson. Pride is so deceptive, it seems so right at the time, that we push reason aside and give in to self-gratification. Growing up poor, we saw so many people (the Joneses!) with new cars and new stuff and we wanted some too. Pride has many faces, but in time it will bring all to their knees in shame. Young children are not self-conscious about their possessions; as long as they are warm and well fed, they are happy!

Pride and Prejudice

There is nothing noble in being superior to your fellow man; true nobility is being superior to your former self.
—Ernest Hemingway

It seems that Americans pride themselves in their individuality and unwavering partisan views when it comes to the north/ south, whites/others, Christian/others, gay/others, Democrats/ Republicans. We can indoctrinate ourselves with our leanings, only reading or listening to certain news outlets and TV and radio programs, and be unaccepting of others. We surround ourselves with those with the same worldview and become paranoid of any thought different from ours. Your associations and media intake have a powerful influence and can mold your thoughts and prejudices. I spent a year in East Cleveland (ninety percent black), where all I heard was black-influenced media and black preachers, and I started to have an attitude with white people. And my mother is white! This shows what media and a closed community can do.

Especially as one gets older, they start to form presuppositions that lead to prejudices, putting people in boxes such as blacks are this, Mexicans are that, gays are this, people in the South are this; people from these colleges are that and so on. To be honest, some stereotypes can have a basis in truth, but there are exceptions to every rule. For me, when I reflect upon my life, right from the beginning it was an uphill battle. My African-American father lived out his stereotype and my mother struggled to raise four kids. To make matters worse, at an early age both sets of grandparents disowned our interracial family. I grew up in Norwich England where it's ninety-nine percent Anglo (white). When we moved into our first section 8 housing (council housing) someone wrote on the front of our house "nigg*** go home" (welcome to the neighborhood!). I was so young I only remember fragments of my childhood but my parents remember it like it was yesterday and it still hurts. These early years can leave an impression on a child and lead them to form a victim worldview. If my life was defined by what the statisticians and psychologists predicted, there would be little hope for me. Quite frankly, I would still be a relational wrecking ball and my offspring wouldn't have a chance because the apple doesn't fall far from the tree. However, there is good news: you can break down any perceived stereotypes people might have of you; you don't have to be the victim, and although people with their presuppositions will have you in a box (that's human nature), by your actions you can prove their assumptions wrong. I've used my hardships to become better, not bitter, and have made some radical changes that I will share later in the book.

We must leave room for the exceptions to the rule or the stereotype and be open to others until they show us something different. By having a prejudging attitude, we automatically close ourselves off to new experiences and learning something from everyone. I was in Dallas for eight years leading a Christian ministry, and there was a member who was slow to accept any friendship. Though I did nothing but encourage his family, his wall was up. The sad part was that our children were the same age and we had so much in common because of similar upbringing. I eventually left there and about a year later I received an email from him apologizing. He expressed that he had experienced abuses from authority in his childhood and it had affected his view of me. I wish we could have connected and I could have shared my victories over my childhood pain. What a wasted opportunity to enrich each other's lives and learn from each other!

In my practice I can help many people who are open to learning or changing, but there are some who are set in their pride. Tony A. Gaskins Jr. puts it eloquently: *"You can't teach someone who thinks they know it all. Help those who want help and let the rest learn the hard way.*

If they refuse to hear it, life will make sure they feel it."

In contrast to our adult relational conundrum and pride, children have no preconceived agenda and all they see is another kid on the slide they want to play with. Children don't see color or political affiliation; they don't see where you were educated, what religion you are or where you live. All they want to do is play and if that child is a bad kid, then they will take their ball and go play with another kid. When it comes to learning, kids just want to drink up life and grow. Children keep life simple. All our hurts from our past and present, all our presuppositions and fears, stop our childlikeness from shining through to new friendships and having new learning experiences.

Consider the Outcome of Their Life

I was at a community college and attending a Family and Marriage class, and the professor had an edge to her voice and a low view of marriage. I was intrigued, so after the class I asked her about her teaching pedigree. To my surprise, without prompting she spoke about her recent divorce and the fact that she wasn't fired up about what she was teaching. It's sad to teach something you don't believe in anymore—what torture! We can be so impressed with those in academia, but behind the PowerPoint their lives are in shambles (they show up at my office). We are so mesmerized by their worldly status and how people praise them. But in life, it seems we neglect what seems mundane: our parents, our kids and our marriage; although these leave the greatest regret, especially when they are gone. Even some major pop stars are only projecting confidence that's not real. I was watching an interview with Lionel Richie, the master of love songs ("Hello," "Still in Love," "Endless Love"), but after the interview I wouldn't seek him out for family and marital advice because of his two divorces and being estranged from his kids—so much for "Endless Love"! If I wanted to write a love song, I would definitely call Lionel (I'm a big fan), but that's it. Can people give advice? Yes, but it's like meeting with an interior designer at their home and it's unfurnished and dirty! No matter what they said you would not hire them. Sometimes we are enamored by people's talent and charisma and want to adopt their worldview, but be careful.

I've worked for a couple of Fortune 500 companies. The top salespeople and executives had the big homes and new Mercedes and went on fancy holidays. As a young, ambitious man I was envious and wanted it too. One day I was out with Rick in his two-seater sports car on a sales call. Rick was the top sales guy in the company but he didn't seem himself; he was agitated. It was only 11 a.m. and I smelled alcohol on his breath. He was very sharp with me and seemed distracted. We were driving down a side street at about 40 mph and out of the blue he decided to pull up the handbrake, hard. The car literally did a bunny hop and flipped on its roof. We were going down the road on the roof at 40 mph! All I can remember is glass smashing, the sound of grinding metal and airbags going off. I was suspended upside down in midair by the seatbelt. As the car ground to a halt, I was dangling by the seatbelt and wondering if I was hurt. I was scared to press the belt release because I could hurt my back or neck. When I did release the seatbelt I put my hand down to limit the impact and cut my hand on glass. Considering the car was written off, I was lucky. As for Rick, he was fine, and he pleaded with me not to tell the police that he had been drinking and had engaged the handbrake while the vehicle was moving. I was so shocked and perplexed at Rick's actions, and before the police arrived, a towing company came and cleaned up the accident. No other people were hurt so it was settled by the insurance company. A couple of days later Rick apologized for his recklessness and told me he had had a drinking problem for a while and that he was losing his wife and kids because of his lack of involvement due to overworking and infidelity. He said the only good thing he had in his life was the work and the accolades from his sales. In my blindness, I had wanted to be like Rick. He was my Fortune 500 corporate superhero, but if I spent the time he did at work and the time away from my wife and kids, I *would* be like him in twenty years!

You must consider the outcome of people's lives and stop falling for what you see on the surface. Many people have superpowers (public speaking, preaching, teaching, singing, sports, rapping, designing or money-making) but I don't want to be them because they are tormented by their own demons. A childlike perspective is to know people and see where they excel and imitate that characteristic or virtue (being a loyal friend, a person of integrity, a truth seeker, faithful to your wife or girlfriend and being there for your kids emotionally and physically). Consider the outcome of their life; if you do what they do, you will have what they have—good and bad!

Student of Life

A true genius admits that he/she knows nothing.
—Albert Einstein

Albert understood that there was more to life than scientific knowledge; he was a student of life. Learning diminishes when we think we know something. It is something that children do, and without it we would still be saying "mama" and "dada" and our writing skills would be limited to scribbling. Children are like sponges: they are thirsty for knowledge and new experiences. There comes a time as an adult when we become educated and have mastered the basics of a career. Now that we have "arrived," we are making money. I have found that when one reaches the age of twenty-five to thirty years, their teachability seems to diminish. How do you know if your learning has diminished? When you stop challenging yourself cognitively and emotionally. One should constantly seek out different genres in reading to stretch oneself and constantly seek out new relationships, especially with people from different cultures.

When I look at my personal formation, it's a colorful canvas, having an English mum, African-American dad, a wife who is Puerto Rican and whose father has Native American origins, and our kids are confused (Native-afro-anglo-Rican)! This diversity has always kept me on my toes and intrigued by different cultures. I've either lived in or visited more than twenty countries from Belize to Ukraine. I have been homeless and I have lived in Beverly Hills. Growing up with no religion, I have studied Daoism, Hinduism, Confucianism, Judaism, Islam (reading the Koran) and Christianity. I have attended five secular and theological colleges and universities and been around some great minds. I still read five to ten books a year on different subjects searching for nuggets of truth. I've rubbed shoulders with millionaires, CEOs of Fortune 500 companies, political figures, pop stars and dynamic preachers and speakers. I embrace all these experiences, but as I said before, the greatest influences that formed me were from the playground with the fights and creating boundaries. It seems weird saying this, but I'm thankful for people like Bob who exploited me, teaching me about evil and unsafe people, and the pain from my childhood has helped me to connect with others in ways I couldn't have without it. The truths of life are what have changed me, but sometimes the hardest lessons in life are the ones that no classroom can teach you.

Part III

Innate and Spiritual Childlikeness

Again, children love learning and embracing new concepts. As we venture into the next section of the book I'm imploring you not to "go adult" on me and shut down! To keep our childlikeness journey going, we must venture into the uncomfortable and unknown. I would not be doing my authorial duty if I just gave you milk and didn't push you on to solid food. In the previous chapters we have examined the scientific, emotional and cognitive fundamentals of childlikeness. The next several chapters will be on the innate and spiritual aspects of childlikeness. Most freak out about anything innate because they can't see it or touch it, but superheroes constantly go into the unknown and always come out victorious.

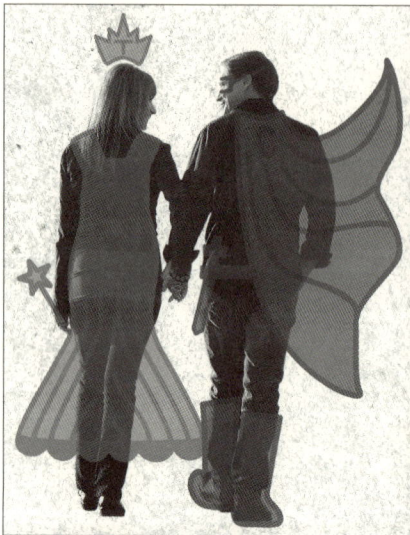

Chapter 11

Our Inner Child Wants to Come Out

When I was young, it seemed that life was so wonderful, a miracle. Oh, it was beautiful, magical.

And all the birds in the trees, well they'd be singing so happily, joyfully, playfully watching me.

But then they sent me away to teach me how to be sensible, logical, responsible, practical.

And they showed me a world where I could be so dependable, clinical, intellectual, cynical.

—Supertramp, "The Logical Song"[6]

What happened to us? In our adulthood we all can become serious. Due to circumstances or poor choices we don't trust anyone anymore and become cynical. If someone looks happy at work, we say that they are not working hard enough because they are not stressed like us. We all are born with innocence and love in our hearts, but for many our upbringing sucked that right out of us. Where did the childlikeness go?

Looking at our culture today, many would say that our society is more perverse and violent as reflected in the current movies and music. When I was a kid, I listened to the Sugar Hill Gang rapping about hanging out with friends, but today it's Lil Wayne rapping about *itches and **ores. The movies that were PG13 didn't have profanity in them or sexual connotations, but today it seems that PG13 movies are hard to watch. I have walked out of some because I felt violated. In the twenty-first century, Hollywood wants to show more gore, violence and sexual content by pushing a more liberal censorship. But you might be surprised to see what the top movies of today are and what content people are craving for.

> ### The WORLDWIDE top ten best-selling movies of all time:
> 1. Avatar
> 2. Titanic
> 3. Harry Potter and the Deathly Hallows Part 2
> 4. Marvel's The Avengers
> 5. Frozen
> 6. Iron Man 3
> 7. Transformers: Dark of the Moon
> 8. Lord of the Rings: The Return of the King
> 9. Skyfall
> 10. Transformers: Age of Extinction

Others movies in the top twenty are *The Dark Knight Rises* (Batman), *Toy Story 3, Jurassic Park, Alice in Wonderland* and *The Lion King*. Even *E.T.* is at #46. You would think all the movies that come out with crude language and sex would be in the top fifty. The closest movie that meets that criterion is *The Hangover Part II*, which is #99! The Disney, Pixar and Marvel series are what dominate the top 100. People around the world are looking for wholesome entertainment. No matter what Hollywood thinks, there is a child in all of us that wants a fun-loving flick. It's like we are fighting to hold on to our childhood memory, and two hours of watching *Toy Story* takes us there. These types of movies are powerful and timeless, like *E.T.* which came out thirty-two years ago!

I must admit, as an adult I have cried over a Disney movie. I feel weird crying over a silly movie, and I make an excuse or hide my tears because I don't want my wife and kids to see my childlikeness. Why do we, especially men, do this? I think it's our inner child trying to bubble up but we suppress these feelings and mask them with adulthood. Most of these top movies reinforce the universal principle of this book, "capes and tiaras," and our ongoing appetite for a childlike narrative.

Okay, Marvin, how about contemporary music; what is the best-selling single in 2014? It must be by Beyoncé, Taylor Swift, Usher or Rihanna. No, the top selling single is "Happy" by Pharrell Williams, taken from the sound track of *Despicable Me 2*. Even while watching the World Cup in Brazil, we heard this song playing in every stadium.

It has become a YouTube phenomenon with people all over the world posting their version of the song and dance moves. Millions of people are refreshed by these songs of innocence instead of the constant diet of crude, sexually charged music. The "Happy" song popularity shows that people around the world crave a childlike happiness.

We may have different languages, cultures and even beliefs (Islam, Christianity, Hinduism and atheism) but we all can connect with that longing to tap into our inner child. Even though my childhood was manic, I remember moments of just being a child, and TV-Y7 shows remind me of that innocence. Unfortunately, we grow up and embrace adulthood, which is calculated, overly serious, untrusting and cynical. Our adulthood can be a reflection of the hurts and poor choices we have made, seen in how we shut down to protect ourselves. Through self-protection from deep emotional hurt we become distrustful and critical of others. This is the very opposite of being childlike, open and trusting.

I'm sitting in Starbucks writing the end of this chapter and there are three guys in their late twenties playing Go Fish, who just asked two random strangers in their mid-thirties to join in. What blasphemy! Keep your childish games to yourself! Starbucks is a professional establishment for business meetings, student study and a $5 coffee! But I'm curious; how will these strangers respond? Will they feel insulted and grab their tall, double-pump pumpkin spice lattes with soy milk and extra whip with froth and leave? No, the two strangers lit up in glee, had a childlike intervention from their adult responsibilities and sat down and played. The joy at that table lit up the whole café. Phew, I'm glad they responded that way; otherwise my whole thesis would be out the window (23,456 words for nothing!). Caution: Childlikeness can break out anywhere at any time!

There is a child in each of us screaming to get out. Consciously or unconsciously, we all have a deep desire to connect with our childlikeness. It seems that we are wired to live out this childlike narrative in our lives.

Chapter 12

Your First Words

"Don't take offense if your baby says dada first; 99.9% of them do," said my pediatrician. He's only had one patient in his practice ever that said "mama" first and that's because she named the bottle "mama" so the baby, reaching for the bottle, would say "mama, mama."

—modernmum.com

Really, mums, after nine months of carrying this child, the aversions to favorite foods, the morning sickness, the back aches, getting up to pee every two hours, then watching your body expand (sometimes it never goes back!), and then the hours of labor and birth. Then for the first several months, with waking up for feedings and the constant care, life becomes a nap and on top of all this is postnatal depression. That child's first words should be "Thank you, mama, for all your sacrifice and love; you are the best mama in the world," but, no, it's "dada"! In this day and age, many dads are not even around. Both of my children started saying "dada" first, and it drove my wife crazy, but I was there in the delivery room holding her hand and giving her ice chips; I put in some effort! Dada forever!

On a more serious note: Why dada? Why not mama? Or baba for a bottle of milk, or yumyum for food; all are easy to say, but our first audible word is "dada." Most kids see food, milk and their mothers more than their fathers, but their first word is "dada"! When I examine the statistical evidence and through my own personal experience, I must ask, is there something going on? We step into a realm that may go beyond mere language development. Just coincidence or, again, are we innately wired? Do we have an inherent yearning for a father, a dada?

I went on You Tube for research and there were 58,000 videos on a child's first word being "dada." Here's one for all the mums out there:

https://www.youtube.com/watch?v=b7nKbl5VoIw

Reflection

In chapters 3, 4 and 5 we looked at the devastating effects on children of a fatherless upbringing. Is there a universal spiritual concept working here beyond our physical realm when it comes to childlikeness and fatherhood? When one examines the names given to the ultimate creator by the major world religions: Para Brahman (Hindu), Allah (Islam), Tian (Taoism), Yahweh (Jews), Christianity is the only one that calls its deity Father. Considering the overwhelming evidence that childlikeness is a necessity in our lives, emotionally, physically and cognitively, could the fatherhood component also need to be examined as well, since all children have a father? I will entertain this theory moving forward.

Chapter 13

Child Protective Services

Protect the Innocent

So far we have pounded on this idea of being like a child, but now we are left vulnerable and exposed to this cruel heartless world, opening ourselves up for more abuse. I have seen my fair share of childhood abuse in my life and the lives of others. While in Dallas, I worked for our local police department in their domestic violence unit and counseled people arrested for domestic crimes. It breaks my heart when innocent children have been neglected or abused (if I wasn't a Christian, I would have taken some of these adults out back and given them a good beating!). These kids are like lambs led to the slaughter. It doesn't seem fair; little children can't defend themselves and don't have a voice. The goal of the department was to first protect the innocent by taking them out of the harmful situation and then find them food, clothing and shelter.

My wife had a challenging childhood. Growing up in a single-parent home, her mother had to work, and at five years old, Sharisse was left alone with her mother's boyfriend.

Here's an excerpt from her book *Because Life Happens*:

> *One day, my mother was at work and as usual, we were alone. For some creepy reason [my mother's boyfriend]} decided to show me an inappropriate device and ask me if I liked it. I knew immediately that something was wrong, but because I was a child,*

I went along with it and said yes. One thing led to another, and he started doing things that he had no business doing to me. He began touching me in an improper fashion, and he even exposed himself to me. I remember being horrified by all of this and quite confused. Sadly, this sexual molestation continued for years. It started when I was five years old and ended when I was twelve. He never told me not to tell. It was just kind of understood that it would be "our little secret." He would offer me money, candy and privileges in return. He would do the vile things he was doing to me and then turn around and try to act like a father by exacting discipline upon me. I was very hostile toward him. I was hoping my mother would ask me why this was so, but unfortunately, she never did.

Sometimes when he would come home from one of his evening jobs, he would crawl into bed with me. His excuse was that my bed was better for his back. I used to love back rubs; in fact, amazingly, I still do. However, he would offer to rub my back for me, and his hands would inevitably end up in places where they should not have been. I don't believe my mother ever insisted that he not sleep in my bed. Maybe she was too young and naïve or possibly in denial about the obvious. Later in life, I even asked my mom if she had suspected that anything weird was going on. After she reflected briefly, she responded, "No." When I asked her about this, I was a mother, and I just could not fathom allowing my boyfriend to sleep in my daughter's bed.... I hated [him] with a passion. I wished him dead many a time. I wished I could cause him intense bodily harm.[7]

This molestation went on for *seven years*! What do you do when people who should be responsible and protect you, do not? When loved ones let us down, how can we trust anyone else? Where is God in all this? How could a loving God let this traumatic thing happen to a five-year-old precious princess? Our childhood can define our worldview, and when it starts like this, we are destined for Victimville or a life of therapy! How one processes this defilement will make them bitter or better. I've known my wife for twenty-five years and have seen her battle her childhood demons. I am proud of her for finding solace in a loving Father, the only father that's truly been in her life. Here's another excerpt from the same chapter in her book:

> *Now I like to think about all that has happened to me as a vehicle that has served to help me become the person I am today. I am at a place in my life where I can share freely about what happened to me. I think that every time I share about my past, I become stronger and stronger. It never fails when I share this portion of my life story at events: Droves of women inevitably come up to me afterward because they, too, have endured such hardship. Many have come to me in tears because they are still in shackles; some have not even begun their journey to heal, while others have been suddenly empowered to begin. It is rather humbling when this happens to me, but I am greatly honored that God now uses me in this way to help many. Who knew! Oh, yeah—God did!*

My wife's story goes against all psychological theory. Most therapists and psychologists would give little hope to a person who goes through several years of sexual abuse and at such an impressionable age. The psychological fallout from her childhood ordeal should have left my wife with a lifelong battle with depression, problems trusting others and slim hope of sustaining functional relationships. Well, with our loving Father all things are possible. His Protective Services elevates us above our dysfunction, our poor choices and the sin of our forefathers and mothers. We can turn other people's sin into God's glory. So many women have been healed because of my wife's healing. She has spoken to many young girls and warned them of the signs of such abuse. Her tiara is shining brighter than ever. She's my queen. Our Father allows hard things to happen to us for the greater good.

The most influential people have gone through tremendous suffering to inspire millions, like Nelson Mandela and Martin Luther King (sometimes the person's death causes the greatest impact). These men experienced many injustices but by embracing God's ethos they brought about change. Jesus' life and death epitomizes these principles. Not only did he change the world but he brought eternal hope to all.

Food, Clothing and Shelter: The Basic Necessities

Another example of God's Child Protective Services in action was in February 2010 when I was frustrated with the predictability of my life. After several conversations with my wife and others, we put in our notice at our ministry job and started praying for God to open doors. I went on a couple of interviews but they didn't pan out. One day I was talking to a friend about someday going back to the UK and starting a church in the "most irreligious city in the UK," my hometown of Norwich. I asked, "Where are we going to get the money from?" and said, "My son has autism" and offered several other excuses. He continued to explain about a nonprofit he had established and how people donated through his website. The wheels started to turn and I shared this idea with my religious as well as nonreligious friends. To my surprise, several of them said that they would give $50 to $100 a month to support the cause. Many Christians said we were crazy, but other doors opened up and we decided to sell everything in our four-bedroom home (see pictures at norwichchurch.org) then left for the UK in August 2010 with ten suitcases, our kids and our cat. What forty-five-year-old man would do this to his wife, eight-year-old daughter and eleven-year-old son with special needs? This kind of stuff is what young people with no responsibilities do! Oh, by the way, we had nowhere to stay, no mission funding or jobs to go to. We had a little savings from what we sold, but no plan B and no rich parents to bail us out; the only parent we had was our Father in heaven.

We flew out on faith and after a twelve-hour flight, we were tired and jetlagged. We arrived at Heathrow airport, but there was a problem: I was a British citizen but my wife and kids were not, and the immigration officer told me at the desk that I could stay but my wife and kids needed to fly back to the USA that very day. Could this be a sign that I'd made a stupid decision? We had sold everything, so they had nothing to go back to! It was my fault; I didn't have the right visas for them, but after a couple of hours of talking (praying) to our Father, they let us in.

For the first month, we slept on people's floors with pillows and airbeds. Finally we found a small 900-square-foot apartment. This was a big adjustment from the 2800-square-foot house we had just left behind. All our furniture was given to us by church members and we bought a car for $500. There was not a month where our income didn't meet our outgoings; we paid all our bills on time and had no debt. Some months we didn't have enough for rent until a donation would come in at the last minute. We were truly dependent on our Father to provide. Over the four years we needed about $300,000 to survive, and we did. God had provided! I reflect on our experience and this passage comes to mind:

> For the pagans run after all these things, and your heavenly **Father knows** that you need them. But seek first his kingdom and his righteousness, **and all these things** will be given to you as well. Therefore do not worry about tomorrow, for tomorrow will worry about itself.[8]
>
> —Jesus

"Seek first his kingdom and his righteousness and all these things will be given to you as well": this passage rings true in our lives. "These things" are our kids, possessions, money, shelter and food. Yes, the Father took care of our marriage, rent, food, jobs and the mission. How about my autistic son? The "Father knows" our needs. For years my son has struggled socially and in school. Our Father has seen our tears and my grieving over my son and us not having a typical father-son relationship, especially in his early years. To be honest, my son continued to struggle in school in the UK, and three schools in two years didn't help, but I held on to God's promises that he would do right by my kids if we did his will. We moved back to the USA a few months ago and were concerned about his transition and his grades. He just got his first-semester grades, and he earned four Bs and one A (with no modifications). Also, when my son was younger we couldn't kick a ball around, because with his autism he couldn't understand basic instructions. This summer he played soccer on a team for under-18s, as he's only fifteen. It was a big learning curve considering he had only been playing for three years. Their team won their summer division, and out of twenty players on the team, the coach selected only four for the state academy program. My son was one of them! Wow, my Father came through on his promise of "all these things." Thanks, Dada; I'm humbled to tears and grateful. Sorry for doubting your love (I will share more about this in Appendix II). I am a full recipient of his Child Protective Services. He protects you and your children too!

Chapter 14

Childlike Purity

A princess wants to save herself for her prince. This is considered an old-fashioned and outdated principle. Many teens and young adults just don't have the emotional maturity to handle an intimate relationship, but many are having sex by sixteen. At that age one is so naïve and has no understanding of the emotional and spiritual fallout of their actions. I have many clients who come into my practice who have had several relationships and are struggling to love the person they are with. When I ask them when they were truly in love they all go back to their first love.

Your first love can be so all-encapsulating that you can't see being with anyone else for the rest of your life. Once bitten by the love bug you say to yourself, "He's the one!" This love is for real and all-consuming, even though you're fifteen and he's an immature seventeen. He's not a virgin but you are, and he's saying he loves you and wants you to be his girlfriend. You swap promise rings and say that you will love each other forever. Your first sexual encounter is at a party with your boyfriend reeking of alcohol; what a way to give something away that you can't get back. There is complete trust and you have no walls up, but after a year he's out with his friends again flirting with some girl. The jealousy is too much and it's over. Your heart is broken and you vow never to love another boy or man that way again. You feel betrayed and the hope of real love has gone for good. When it comes to new relationships a wall of mistrust is now in place. Here's a story of someone's first love experience:

I lost my virginity with a guy from my class I was in love with. I was 18 years old. I had a crush on him since first grade. He was out of reach until we started joking about it. Then I asked him what if things [went] there and so, the next day we met up.

It was also his first time, so it was our first time.... The weirdest part was [after] we did it, we got out of the car and we both went our separate ways. I told him, "See ya on Monday at school!" And that was it.... The only sad thing is that we weren't even friends.
— Anonymous, Huffington Post.com

The power of fantasizing about love and falling in love with love can cloud your judgment. This poor girl who was so desperate for affection gave herself to a stranger in the back of a car. Society and media say random sex is magical and romantic, but experiences like this tell a different story.

Here's another story about someone's first love:

I started dating him my sophomore year of high school. He called me up on the phone one night out of nowhere and asked me to go to Homecoming with him. I had never talked to him before in my life but I had seen him and I thought he was cute. That was the beginning of the greatest love of my life.

Mama didn't like the idea of me going to Homecoming with him. I was 15 and he was almost 19. I guess she saw how excited I was about going with him and decided it would be okay. The next week he picked me up from school one day because we decided we should probably spend some time together first and get to know each other. This guy really warmed my heart and put butterflies in my stomach. From the first moment he grabbed my hand I knew I loved him.

We went to Homecoming together that Saturday. He was so handsome. After that we spent all of our time together. We had to deal with all the typical teenage jealousy stuff but it still didn't change the fact that we really loved each other.

After nine short months the time had come for us to take the relationship to the next level. I was a virgin and I am still under the impression that he was one also, but was never really clear on that. We made love on the couch in my living room....

We were great for a year after that. We were perfect for each other. There comes an end to love that young though. By the time I was 18 years old so much had changed. I was growing up. I saw so much to life. I wanted to be free to enjoy all the stuff that I knew he wouldn't let me enjoy. I needed to be able to date other guys and go out with my friends. It was a need, not a want. If we would have gotten married then we would not have lasted.

Then there comes regret. I am going to be 24 next week. I have already been married and divorced once. I've dated plenty of guys by now. I am tired of going out with my friends…. No guy has ever loved me as much as he did. He told me that would happen. I've never loved anyone as much as I love him. He also told me that would happen. I miss him. I want him to hold me in his arms again. I want to hear his voice.

—Anonymous, "I Miss My First Love"

This woman depicts my hypothesis. Now she is in a bind. She has regret and baggage and the possibility of a deep loving relationship in the future is slim. As men can be reckless, women can too!

A first love is a pivotal relationship. Most don't go well and a shadow of a person is left afterwards. As we get older we play games (as I did) or keep our guards up. Hence, it gets harder to find love because of all the baggage and fears we have. Love can only be found when two people are giving 100%, creating a safe environment in which to grow emotionally and spiritually. Some people have the propensity to give their all to a later relationship, but most don't. Many only have one love in them and after that they are broken, damaged people. When these broken people come together and get married they settle for half-love and are just happy that the spouse comes home, pays some bills and gives hugs sometimes.

"For this reason a man will leave his father and mother and be united to his wife, and they will become one flesh."[9] Our loving Father is not trying to stop us from expressing our sexual freedom but to save us from a fragmented existence. If we may only have one love in us, we need to make sure it's the right one. There must be a commitment, a marriage, before giving yourself. Our heavenly Father knows what's best for us and doesn't want us to be damaged by an immature fling. You might be the one that can love again after heartbreak, but as a dad, I'm not into my daughter taking a chance on the relationship roulette wheel. Her heart is too fragile for that.

Frog DNA

Here is an alarming scientific fact: two becoming one flesh is not only emotional and spiritual but can be through our DNA! DNA is the building block of life, and men have the X and Y chromosome while women have only the X chromosome. It has been widely known that the only way women can have the Y chromosome is by having a child that is a boy. However, immunologists at the Fred Hutchinson Cancer Center in 2004, tested 120 women who had never had a child, and they found the Y chromosome in their DNA. The scientists were baffled, but after examining the women's lifestyles and sexual partners, from their findings it was concluded that through intercourse alone there is a potential for women to hold onto male genes and DNA within their organs and bloodstream for their entire life! Wow, so random acts of meaningless, drunken sex can stay with me for more than one night? Yes. Many women feel that having three or four sexual partners until they find the right one is acceptable. But you could be carrying around not only the emotional baggage from those frogs, but also their slimy DNA, which you could pass on to your future offspring. Looking at the scientific evidence gives a whole new meaning to "one flesh." Remember that you are a princess and that the vetting process is essential to keep the royal bloodline pure.

Our Father Knows Best

Marriage is to protect the princess. Men struggle with commitment and would love to have all the relational benefits without the responsibility. An uncommitted relationship with kids and extensive financial responsibilities leaves a princess vulnerable. When the relationship has no marital commitment, it's easier for a man to walk out on it, especially when emotionally and financially overwhelmed. I have lost count of how many married couples have come to my office and said that if they were not married they would not have sought counseling but just walked away from each other. The vows that they made to each other meant something, and in a last-ditch effort they seek counseling to see if their marriage is salvageable. I would say ninety percent of married couples in crisis who went through the whole counseling process turned things around and are in a better place. When I'm dealing with partnerships or long-term dating couples, it is harder to assess the seriousness of their relationship, because there is no defining moment of oneness in the form of a commitment and vows. My success rate with these types of relationships drops significantly. Here's a statistic to back up my thesis: only twenty-five percent of families out of wedlock stay together; it jumps to seventy-five percent when the parents are married (Daily Mail online). Marriage protects the princesses because they are the ones normally left raising the kids, making them less desirable for future relationships, while the man goes on living his single existence and being a dad two days a week. And we have not even brought up the short-term and long-term fallout on the innocent kids or how they interpret this separation!

Our heavenly Father knows all this and insists on marriage before intimacy. Again, marriage protects women from the uncommitting character flaws of a man. Commitment, commitment, commitment! Remember: When Sharisse made serious boundaries about our sex life, I had the choice to move on and find another victim or get right with Jesus. Princesses, you have more power than you think!

Chapter 15

Two Latchkey Kids Find Love!

So Marvin, you were a horrible person! You were a thief, a cheat, unfaithful to women, an emotional and mental manipulator, violent, heartless, homeless and fatherless. What happened to you that your life would make a 180-degree turn? Religion was the furthest thing from my radar, and at the time I was dating a model and living in Beverly Hills. Even though I was so far from home, there was a hole in my life; I didn't have a father and I would drink myself to sleep to suppress my demons. Not having a role model or a home to go to had opened me up to being abused by people like Bob. By this time, my own poor choices had caught up to me. Deep down, I was completely disenchanted by life and people, even though it seemed that I had everything. I was hard-hearted. To protect myself I used people and had no real friends. Fun for me was crude sarcasm and hurting people with mind games. I wanted people to feel the way I did, and dishing out cutting remarks in some sick way made me feel better. I especially used women for money and self-seeking enjoyment. My childlike heart was long gone, and there seemed to be no redemption in sight. When I met Sharisse, she was nineteen and I was twenty-four. She was another lamb to be added to my slaughter! I had three other girlfriends but she didn't know and I didn't care. I was excited by the deceit and playing with their emotions, a sick entertainment. Sharisse was smitten with me. I was funny, fit and had a cute British accent, but I was a foreign monster. We had been dating for eighteen months, then she started to change.

Here is an excerpt from my first book, *Baguette Moments*:

> One day at a modeling shoot, Sharisse was reached out to by another model who was a Christian. They started a friendship and Sharisse began to go to church and study the Scriptures. I thought it was cute that she was doing the "church thing," until it began affecting my life! Sharisse would study the Scriptures with the church women, and then come back and try to change me. She asked me to stop swearing, but having no fear of God, I cursed even more! But one day, after a Bible study, Sharisse's new conviction not to have sex outside of marriage was "the straw that broke the camel's back" for me. When she told me, "We can't have sex anymore," that was the deal breaker!
>
> This "church thing" had gone too far. Consequently, we broke up, which obviously broke Sharisse's heart. At this point, I did not trust my parents, women or other men. I had no friends—or God. My worldview was confirmed: No one can be completely trusted. I barely even trusted myself, especially when I was drinking. I had reached a crossroads. After a few days passed, I realized that I really missed Sharisse, even though I had other female relationships. So I called her, and she pleaded with me to visit her church.
>
> Visiting Sharisse's church was not a good experience initially. My first inclination was actually to try and take her out of the church! To no one's surprise, I was extremely cynical and critical of everything and everyone there. One of the ministers eventually invited us over for dinner and asked me if I had any questions. I said, "Yes! Why can't we have sex?!" This is a hard question to answer for someone who does not believe the truths found in the Bible.
>
> In the ensuing weeks, God started to soften my heart and open my eyes. I began to notice the sincere friendships and devoted marriages in the church. For me, this made the Bible real, and this realization encouraged me to study the Scriptures. My Bible studying began on a Monday, and by the following Sunday, April 28, 1991, I was baptized near Santa Monica Pier.

The moment when my life changed radically was when I finally had a Father that was forever present—a "Dada" who was always there for me—and the promise of an eternal home. For this transformation to happen, I had to face my hurts and demons and let my heavenly Father's love transform me. I told Sharisse about my deceit and cheating with three other women, and to this day she has never used it against me. She could see my brokenness and repentance. We felt the Father's forgiveness and his love. We started dating as a prince and princess with the purity of children, with no kissing or inappropriate touching, and the trust and integrity was built up in our relationship. No wonder she wore her tiara coming down the aisle! In her heavenly Father's eyes she was pure and holy.

Twenty-three years later, I have been loyal to one woman and am now bringing up our children with the kind of love that we never had growing up. We were broken with lies, deceit, domestic neglect and sexual childhood abuse. Our gentle Father picked up these broken pieces and made us one.

What Does a Childlike Superhero Look Like?

A superhero is gallant and a man of integrity (no games). He is a GENTLEman; he's sensitive and considerate but also in his nature he protects everyone from the bad guys and evil. He can step into the role of being a hero; he's also comfortable sitting behind the desk at *The Daily Planet* editing an article on a cat stuck in a tree! He is flexible to what is needed and is always looking for ways to empower other people's gifts and get them involved. This superhero is fun-loving, spontaneous and responsible. He respects princesses and will not turn into a "carnal lust beast" when he has an interest. He cares for others and is constantly looking for new relationships and opportunities to help. He lives a faithful life and takes conflict head on, resolving any rifts. He feels indignation against unrighteousness and has a personal standard that he holds to. He is constantly growing emotionally and spiritually, becoming more selfless.

The married superhero oversees and protects his family physically, emotionally and spiritually. He has a finger on the pulse of their changing emotional needs. His wife is secure because she feels that she is his number-one priority in the family; she feels cherished and loved. His goal is to save his family first before the world. Sometimes his role is mundane and menial, but love has many gears, even helping his kids tie their shoelaces. As a married superhero, he never puts away his cape and gets comfortable. As he gets older, he is wiser and more organized and therefore uses his time efficiently to continue good deeds and empower others. He still loves to have fun and can surprise you from time to time. He passes on to his son how one should treat a princess by letting him see this in his parents' relationship. His daughter is seeing how a superhero treats a princess and would not accept anything less in her life. A superhero has a perfect balance of compassion and passion.

What Does a Childlike Princess Look Like?

A princess understands that she is royalty and will not lower or degrade herself to anyone or anything. Her dress is stylish and tasteful. Her speech is eloquent and she would not gossip or malign others. She loves laughter and singing because her heart is full of joy and innocence. She loves to be free and daydream about her true love. She will not permit paupers or street urchins in her court. She will not allow the first boy who says, "Oh baby, baby" to woo her; she sees their game a mile off. When it comes to a relationship, she understands the devastation that can happen in an unhealthy "first love" scenario. A princess pays careful attention to her potential prince's character, watching for respect and integrity and noticing his family and relationship dynamics. She is aware of the lust monster that preys on naïve princesses! Her vetting process includes serious spiritual, emotional and sexual boundaries. She has convictions to hold out for her prince, her superhero, and would rather be alone with her heavenly Father than associate with paupers. A princess's tiara dazzles because of her wisdom (her hard head) and purity (her soft, pure heart).

The queen (the married princess) is soft spoken and wise beyond her years. She supports her superhero husband in everything, but if she disagrees she expresses herself in a clear and controlled manner. She respects her husband and will not malign him in front of the kids or friends. She has a pride for her palace; she's hospitable and makes everyone feel welcome. She has a faithful outlook and doesn't succumb to the fears outside her palace walls. She teaches her daughter how to be a princess and her son to be a gentleman. She still wants to be romanced and loves spontaneous fun and surprises. The queen is stunning because of her stature, her eloquence of speech and her respect for her king.

Part IV

Deeper Spiritual Truths

Congratulations; if you have no real belief in God or spiritual concepts and you have managed to read this far then I commend you; you are my hero and you have shown great childlike qualities. The next part of this book is going to delve deeper into theological truths. In this section we are going to examine where Jesus, the Holy Spirit and the Church fit into the metanarrative of childlikeness. I would advise nonbelievers to skip over this section and continue on to Appendices I and II).

Chapter 16

Abba, Father

The 33-Year-Old Child

Jesus, the Son of God, had a close relationship with his Father (like all fathers and sons should) and it is shown throughout the Scriptures. Jesus brought an intimacy to his relationship with God that no Jew had experienced before. The Jews were afraid to even mention the name of Yahweh! Jesus taught his disciples to pray to God as their Father. This would have seemed irreverent to them. It must have been a monumental theological adjustment to go from this God of the Old Testament that destroyed Sodom and Gomorrah with fire and judgment, to a conscientious Father. From the fact that Jesus refers to God as his Father, one can sense a bond of love and trust. This total trust would ultimately lead to his death. The only time Jesus felt separated from his Father was when he took on the sins of man at the cross, crying, "My God, My God, why have you forsaken me?" Jesus always felt a spiritual and emotional connection to his Father and fought to keep that bond even if the strain meant sweating blood.

How did Jesus view his Father? There is one passage that encapsulates this:

> He took Peter, James and John along with him, and he began to be deeply distressed and troubled. **"My soul is overwhelmed with sorrow to the point of death,"** he said to them. "Stay here

and keep watch."

> *Going a little farther, he fell to the ground and prayed that if possible the hour might pass from him. "**Abba, Father**," he said, "everything is possible for you. Take this cup from me. Yet not what I will, but what you will."*

—Mark 14:33–36, emphasis added

In this passage, we find Jesus in the Garden of Gethsemane facing his final hours before the cross. He is wrestling in prayer over his ultimate betrayal, the false accusations from the religious leaders of the day (the Pharisees), then the pending brutality of the Roman soldiers leading to his torturous death. On top of all this, the twelve with whom he had spent three years would all leave him despite their adamant vows to protect him even at the cost of their own lives. During this time of being intensely overwhelmed, Jesus sweat blood. What would any man say or do in this intense situation? Jesus yells out, "*Abba*, Father." The word *abba* means dada in Aramaic. In Jesus' time of need he cries out, "Dada"! Jesus was a grown man, but his love and desire for his dada couldn't be suppressed.

As we develop, our progression of our paternal relationship goes from dada to daddy, then dad, and if we are really formal, we say "father." Dada is the term that a 1-year-old would use. When you are a toddler you trust your parents and they are in total control of your survival (food, clothing and love). A toddler is a liability to themselves: they can't walk straight. Jesus wasn't playing when he really understood his limitations in the flesh and the true power of God. Here's another passage to show this: "*I tell you the truth, the Son can do nothing by himself; he can do only what he sees his Father doing, because whatever the Father does the Son also does*" (John 5:19).

Jesus could do "nothing" without his Father! I think that this is an indication of Jesus' childlikeness. He is an adult, but inside of him is a little child of God. Jesus never lost his place with and childlike affection for his Father. He looked at life as a 1-year-old would. He was thirty-three years old with the heart of a little child.

Is this how you view your existence, that you can do "nothing" without our Father? Are your thoughts, "I can't breathe, walk, talk or drive my car without God!"? If this is how you view yourself before

God, you pray about everything because you realize your need for help and don't take anything for granted. This worldview changes everything. Once realizing this, we are connecting by that same paternal bond that Jesus had with his dada. I believe most Christians miss this intimate connection that is displayed between Jesus and God, and so they suffer and end up living a subpar existence inside the church.

How do you view your relationship with God? Is he the Jehovah God who is scary and punishing, who fills you with unhealthy fear and guilt? When you approach God as your Father, is he your Father, with whom you are only formal and obedient, or is he Dada, a Father who is intimate and nurturing and who will wipe away your tears when you have a booboo? This principle of childlikeness is crucial for one to have a realistic view of their humanistic limitations and to live a life of childlike joy. Again, without a toddler spiritual outlook it's impossible to live the Christian life to its fullest; then and only then can we tap into all of God's Child Protective Services.

I believe Jesus' first word was "Dada" and his last word before the cross was "Dada." When was the last time you said "Dada" to God? If you can't say it, then you are probably not living it! Try it in your prayers and say it in public instead of saying "God" or "Father." Is God, your God, Father or Dada to you?

Chapter 17

Like a Little Child

"Therefore, whoever **humbles himself like this child** *is the greatest in the kingdom of heaven."*
—Jesus, in Matthew 18:4, *emphasis added*

"I tell you the truth, anyone who will not receive the kingdom of God **like a little child** *will never enter it."*
—Jesus, in Mark 10:15, *emphasis added*

According to Jesus the Son of God, Christian childlikeness is a salvation issue. Unless we humble ourselves and become like little children, the Kingdom of Heaven's doors are closed to us! Without reading any other scripture we can draw from our own childhood and make the appropriate changes because we were all children at one time. Therefore, we are without excuse. When I reflect on my childhood, I remember being joyful, I was quick to forgive, I lived in the present and I trusted that my parents would feed me and provide shelter.

When we are baptized, we are childlike: we feel the forgiveness, we want to learn, and God is our *abba*, our dada. During the first few months we grow. We go through new-Christian classes and studies and learn the church's expectations of its members. We make some new friends, get settled in, and after a while, once we see what the minimum expectations are, we think we know the ropes. We lose the desire and personal drive to go beyond the basic "milk" teachings and the tenacity to understand the essence of Christ: his love for the unlovable, his patience, his forgiveness. At this point we can reach a ceiling spiritually and stop growing. I call this becoming a teen: still a child of God but not with the mind of a toddler. Most of us would admit that we are a child of God, but a child of what age? As a spiritual teen, we have a say in what happens in God's household and can critique the leadership. In adolescence, teachability decreases as one gets older and ageism creeps in. We will learn or accept advice only from people whom we admire, are more qualified than we are or have longer tenure than we do. If you hear of an injustice or wrongdoing when you are a teen, you are big enough to defend yourself and others, but slowly the fear and doubts seep in. We become an adult again, cynical and critical of others. That childhood joy and humility are a distant memory. Now, it's five times harder to reconnect with our inner child. If this continues we will forfeit our salvation. Satan knows if that childlike heart is destroyed, we are spiritual toast! When a teenage heart sets in we must look to Jesus in the Garden of Gethsemane, get on our knees and cry out, "*Abba*, Father!"

By your actions: What age child of God are you? A little child or a teen?

A Childlike Heart

> *My son, pay attention to what I say;*
> *listen closely to my words.*
> *Do not let them out of your sight,*
> *keep them within your heart;*
> *for **they are life to those who find them***
> *and health to a man's whole body.*
> ***Above all else, guard your heart,***
> *for it is the wellspring of life*
> —Proverbs 4:20–23, *emphasis added*

How many times while watching a TV program have you had to pause or change the channel because your child walked into the room? This has happened to me several times. I change the channel because I know the content is not child friendly. However, if I am aspiring to attain a childlike heart, I must be conscious of what I consume from movies, music and TV at all times. I have seen many people become numb to what they are watching and listening to. They will even sing out loud the chorus of a song that promotes ungodly living or tell their friends to watch a program that glorifies an immoral life style!

An adult with a childlike heart and a child should be watching the same things. We shouldn't be watching "adult" material, because it violates our childlike hearts with its graphic violence, profanity and sexual content (Proverbs 11:20). Just recently, I decided that the only movies I would watch are fun or inspirational ones. In the past, I felt violated and wanted to take a spiritual shower after watching some of the movies I had chosen to watch. My wife and I have walked out of several movies because they violated our consciences. With that wonderful tool, the Internet, we can now do the research on content before seeing a movie. This is a great, proactive resource. As Christians we must go above and beyond to protect our childlike hearts, because they are delicate things.

Above all else, guard your heart, for it is the wellspring of life.

Brother-Sister Interactions

We must also guard our hearts in our spiritual relationships. We are brothers and sisters in Christ and must be conscious of each other's hearts. If we view each other as God sees us, as children, we will treat each other differently, especially when it comes to conduct in the church. If we are little children of God, we have sensitive hearts that can be violated easily. What we say and do to each other can have an effect on our childlikeness and personal purity. One of the most debated relational dynamics in the church is dating. How should a dating couple act? What is acceptable intimacy for that couple? Here's a scripture to help us: *"Treat younger men as brothers, older women as mothers, and younger women as sisters, with absolute purity"* (1 Timothy 5:1–2).

Take this scripture to heart in a dating situation and ask yourself, "Would I touch my physical mother or sister in that way or would I make sexual comments to my sister or mother?" If you can't say it or do it to your physical mother, sister, father or brother, you probably shouldn't say it to your spiritual one either. Just thinking of touching my mother or sister in an inappropriate way makes me feel nauseous! This is how our Father feels when one has incestuous conduct or feelings with their spiritual siblings, the children of God! We would be horrified if this happened in our physical family; how much more in the family of God? But many in our churches sit back and watch the spiritual incest before their eyes and say nothing.

Men are visually stimulated, and women are stimulated by words and smells that evoke emotion. Men can be oblivious to these emotional triggers and can make a woman struggle or believe that there's a marital future. Every princess dreams of their "happily ever after." When a "Prince Charming," or in reality a frog, opens up this fairytale door with careless sentiments but doesn't have the character to back up a long-term commitment, it can have a destructive effect on a princess's tender heart. Remember, God will hold us accountable for every careless word (Matthew 12:36).

This effect doesn't always come out physically. As a counselor, I have dealt with many emotional affairs formed over Facebook and chat sites, with the participants never having met in person. This shows the power of emotional and cognitive intimacy.

We as children of God, with our delicate hearts, must guard each other and keep spiritual, mental, emotional and physical purity at the forefront. These childhood and family principles are something we all know, because we were children at one point. You don't need a ten-step purity program or an extensive exegetical Bible study on purity to know what's right! Many use the term WWJD—What would Jesus do? Here's a new one: WIDTTMS—would I do this to my (physical) sister?

Chapter 18

The Orphanage

Institutionalized children [in orphanages] exhibit everything from reduced IQs to reductions in brain size and activity... Researchers say that although any time spent in non-family situations is harmful, their work suggests institutionalization past the age of 2, and in some cases earlier, causes irreversible effects.
—Meghan Collins Sullivan, globalpost.com

From the 1960s to the 1980s, the Romanian government came up with an idea that to help communism, every family should have five or more kids. However, families could not support that amount of children and thousands of kids ended up on the streets. The government built orphanages to house the homeless children. The system was overwhelmed, so four or five kids would be assigned to a standard crib with only enough room between the cribs to prop up the babies' coke bottles with nipples on the end filled with milk. The orphanages were so understaffed that the only care that these children received was feeding and diaper changes (if they wore one). They received no love, no hugs and no playtime. The lasting effect of this neglect was profound. These kids were socially challenged and had problems connecting with normal kids. The conditions of the orphanages became so damaging socially and emotionally that some said they might have been better off living homeless on the streets.

The Romanian government thought that their policies and

pouring millions of dollars into this program would help their nation to gain status in Europe, but unfortunately their system was flawed. This is a sad scenario, when an institution puts so much energy and money into protecting and nurturing children but the outcome is a lot less than expected. Why do I use this illustration? I feel like the traditional church structure can be more like an orphanage than a conduit for empowerment and helping people to express their God-given giftedness. Here are several examples of what I've witnessed as a minister, counselor and theological student.

The Disillusioned Orphan

Recently, I spoke to my friend Terry. When I first met him sixteen years ago, he was a confident (some would even say arrogant) MIT graduate student with a new sports car and a new wife. He was doing the best he could for someone in his mid-twenties. He and his wife became Christians. They were very active and aspiring to lead in the church. When we spoke, I hadn't seen him for twelve years. As we started off with pleasantries and shallow talk, he told me about his family, his high-powered management job at a Fortune 500 company, the new cars and the four-bedroom house. All the physical signs of success seemed good. Digging deeper, I asked him how he was doing spiritually. He started to divulge how poorly he had been doing for several years now and how it was affecting his marriage and family. As the physical façade came down, I saw him hunched over and was shocked at how spiritually emaciated he was. He continued by telling me that he was going through the motions and doing the minimum to get by at church: attending all the meetings, giving some money and attending conferences. Emotionally and spiritually he was an orphan; frightened, alone and disillusioned. Where did his confidence go and what went wrong, considering all the aspirations he had at the beginning?

I wanted to know more about his spiritual formation and what happened over the years, since he started with great dreams but now was uninspired and discouraged about all church things. He told me that at work he was inspired by doing multimillion-dollar presentations to top executives, but in the church he was not leading his family spiritually or emotionally or even doing basic Bible studies with anyone. There's something wrong here! Terry and others like him with an established gift-set get baptized, but there's little intentional personal development proportional to and based on their giftedness, and so they keep drinking milk (basic teachings). Terry and others like him start off with great plans for God to do amazing things with their newly transformed life, but all they get are milk-toast new-Christian classes. Then after these new-Christian classes end, their Christianity boils down to reading their Bible daily, coming to church meetings and giving money. However, they have the drive and ability to do so much more. Some come up with faithful ideas but are shut down because they are "too young in the faith." Seeing no opportunities to lead and to do great things for God, they become disenchanted. Once excited about what God can do with them, as the months go by they put their skills back into the world where they feel there is appreciation and room for advancement. The secular workplace has been trained to empower their staff to get the most out of the workforce. The world understands keeping their employees inspired, therefore they spend millions on this a year to accomplish their goals. Terry, after the initial excitement in Christ, kept getting a diet of milk from the church. It seemed that the general populace was happy with milk, that is, the same basics taught over and over again. Terry became a disillusioned orphan at church but in the corporate world a superhero executive making a difference!

Orphan Enabling

Another church dynamic that retards is over-coddling or doing the thinking for people. With coddling, in an act of love we want to show them the life of Christ and we start by helping them with their decision-making. After a while, they become dependent on it. Sometimes it is easier to tell someone to do something than to spend the hours it takes to teach them. Eventually this dynamic puts a lot of pressure on those doing the enabling and it paralyzes the enabled. The person needing constant direction becomes inept at making basic life decisions and spiritual decisions. They need help about basic life endeavors such as balancing their checkbook, getting or holding a job, paying bills on time, etc. Spiritually, they have to be reminded to read their Bible daily, serve the poor and share their faith, which are all spiritual but elementary teachings. This keeps them in spiritual diapers for years. After being in the church for five to ten years, these people have trouble relating to common folk. Many Christians have spent more years in church than in the world, but their lives don't show it and they still struggle with basic life skills in their thirties and forties. They have the same life and spiritual skills as they did ten years earlier and continue to live mediocre and ineffective lives.

> *In fact, though by this time you ought to be teachers, you need someone to teach you the elementary truths of God's word all over again. You need milk, not solid food! Anyone who lives on milk, being still an infant, is not acquainted with the teaching about righteousness.*
>
> —Hebrews 5:12–13

When a person has spent years on milk they become accustomed to it, so when someone comes along with solid food they throw a baby tantrum and can get really mean. In the past I've confronted these people and they have threatened my life (and in Texas they have guns!). It's sad when you want to enrich people's lives and they respond in such a way that even my wife is scared to leave the house.

For a church to be healthy it must have more solid-food eaters than milk-drinkers, but most churches fit the 80/20 rule: 20% of the people do 80% of the work. So, if we have a church of 200, that's 160 drinking milk. However, that twenty percent may not be mature although they are active in helping with church events. Then take into account all of the events on the calendar (most of them the same as the year before) that need organizing, and who has the time to walk with the babies and immature? Many evangelical churches want to grow each year but only to add more people to the milk line. It looks good at the national and regional conferences and on the stat sheets but not for the twenty percent and the staff! The numbers and events supersede maturation of the saints. As a father and a husband, I would never consider adding another child to our family if we were not able to love the ones we already have; it would be considered too reckless and irresponsible. Actually, CPS would take all my kids away because of the neglect, so how much more the children of God! Jesus was into maturing what God gave him and spent three years with the Twelve, walking with them and loving them.

So in the milk-driven church, we have an orphanage situation with five babies to one crib trying to help each other. Just like the homeless kids, they are happy to get off the streets but end up in an orphanage where after some years, they become institutionalized and have spent most of their life having others thinking for them and coddling them so they become cowardly (Revelation 21:8), timid, overwhelmed by even the basics, socially unrelatable and feeling ineffective in the church with no aspirations or opportunities for greatness. Then the question must be asked, are they better off than they would have been on the streets?

"When an evil spirit comes out of a man, it goes through arid places seeking rest and does not find it. Then it says, 'I will return to the house I left.' When it arrives, it finds the house unoccupied, swept clean and put in order. Then it goes and takes with it seven other spirits more wicked than itself, and they go in and live there. And the final condition of that man is worse than the first."
—Matthew 12:43–45

The streets are tough but they mold your character and in a harsh way refine you to take care of yourself. There are only two people mentioned in the Bible whose faith amazed Jesus: one is the centurion and the other the Canaanite woman. Why? Because of their tenacity. They weren't Christians but had character and street smarts from life's hard knocks. Unless disciples develop God-given character, we fail them. We want our brothers and sisters to be sound in their faith, but stopping the pain of personal development will keep them in a constant embryonic state.

Once a little boy was playing outdoors and found a fascinating caterpillar. He carefully picked it up and took it home to show his mother. He asked his mother if he could keep it, and she said he could if he would take good care of it. The little boy got a large jar from his mother and put plants to eat, and a stick to climb on, in the jar. Every day he watched the caterpillar and brought it new plants to eat. One day the caterpillar climbed up the stick and started acting strangely. The boy worriedly called his mother who came and understood that the caterpillar was creating a cocoon.

The mother explained to the boy how the caterpillar was going to go through a metamorphosis and become a butterfly. The little boy was thrilled to hear about the changes his caterpillar would go through. He watched every day, waiting for the butterfly to emerge. One day it happened, a small hole appeared in the cocoon and the butterfly started to struggle to come out. At first the boy was excited, but soon he became concerned. The butterfly was struggling so hard to get out! It looked like it couldn't break free! It looked desperate! It looked like it was making no progress! The boy was so concerned he decided to help. He ran to get scissors, and then walked back (because he had learned not to run with scissors...). He snipped the cocoon to make the hole bigger and the butterfly quickly emerged!

As the butterfly came out the boy was surprised. It had a swollen body and small, shriveled wings. He continued to watch the butterfly expecting that, at any moment, the wings would dry out, enlarge and expand to support the swollen body. He knew that in time the body would shrink and the butterfly's wings would expand. But neither happened!

The butterfly spent the rest of its life crawling around with a swollen body and shriveled wings.

It never was able to fly...

As the boy tried to figure out what had gone wrong his mother took him to talk to a scientist from a local college. He learned that the butterfly was SUPPOSED to struggle. In fact, the butterfly's struggle to push its way through the tiny opening of the cocoon pushes the fluid out of its body and into its wings. Without the struggle, the butterfly would never, ever fly. The boy's good intentions hurt the butterfly.

—Author unknown

God wants all of his children to fly. Get out of the way and let the natural process of his refinement do its work. Yes, it's painful to watch, but it's the only way to learn to fly! There is good pain and bad pain, and persevering and growing comes with good pain. Through this learning process of tough love, God's child will learn right from wrong. Sometimes they need to get back on the streets to understand good and evil like I did with Bob. Later they are convicted by their stupidity and it turns into conviction. Then they become an advocate of change for others. No pain, no conviction.

"Perseverance must finish its work so that you may be mature and complete, not lacking anything" (James 1:4, *emphasis added*). James's commission to the church is for everyone to be "mature and complete," not just the twenty percent. Thinking for people or clipping the wings of those who want to fly will retard God's children. It's all about walking with people and forming Christ in them, and sometimes that means doing nothing and leaving room for God, just as in the prodigal story the father had to let his son go. People should depend on God, not solely on man. Again, maturity is the goal, and if this is not happening one must examine their process of discipleship.

As a parent, I don't want my kids living with me in their thirties. I would have failed them in preparing them for life. My children have different personalities and gifts; I have to be on my toes, adjusting my parenting style and staying emotionally connected with them as they navigate through the volatility of adolescence. I have to constantly adapt to mature them and mold their character, and sometimes that means letting them go to find out for themselves. One size doesn't fit all! Too much coddling leads to an inept child, too much control leads to rebellion, and lack of empowerment leads to disenchantment.

How about with the children of God; what program or class can we go to in order to get this type of mentorship? How can we take care of the eighty percent? This only happens when all of us are equipped with the loving tools of Jesus and we care about spiritual maturity more than any calendar item. Again, Jesus spent three years with the twelve apostles.

Preachers and Orphanage Directors

I've led mission teams and churches of twenty to several hundred over the last twenty-plus years, so I understand the stresses of the ministry, and at times it felt like I was running an orphanage! Most preachers have good hearts and have given up lucrative careers to go into the ministry. They get into ministry and realize the amount of needs there are and that few care or are equipped, just like the orphanage director who is overwhelmed by all the children and can only take care of their essential needs. Due to this ongoing demand they feel stretched to spend quality time with people and really nurture them to maturity in Christ. Many a preacher whom I admired when I was a young minister because of their teaching and ministry building, is now divorced or their kids don't believe! Some of them got consumed in the never-ending need cycle of ministry and reached a stage of burnout, and their families, friendships and health suffered from all the needs in the fellowship.

> *Pastors...are pressured by the responsibilities of their position.... Some of their common concerns:...80% say their ministry has had a negative impact on their children, 70% struggle with depression, 71% are having financial difficulty, 65% have thought recently about giving up on ministry, and 70% say they do not have a close friend.*
>
> —Rob Bell, preacher

Ministers are children of God too! They hurt and struggle with life as you do. If we looked at each other as children, I think we'd find a common bond and a greater compassion for each other. Being a minister, people come to you for their problems and don't ask how you are doing. This is a double-edged sword: we like the influence we have on a congregation and people looking to us for guidance. It makes us feel wanted, but if we are the only one they listen to or get direction from, we end up giving a little to a lot and no one is really happy. There are only two ways to go in a milk-driven ministry: 1) care and be overwhelmed by the needs or 2) institutionalize and manage the masses.

In most of the larger churches the minster has to stay behind the pulpit and not go into the crowd because he doesn't want to be barraged with needs or make promises he can't keep, so he hides behind corporate ministry busyness (having meetings and arranging events) and "larger ministry responsibilities," only to avoid intimate fellowship and become like a politician shaking hands and kissing babies. Then there's a lot of pressure on the pulpit to move the church, but it's like a shotgun affect. Some get hit and learn while others don't. Preachers get frustrated with the individuals who don't respond, yet many of those individuals want to do more for Christ but are stuck emotionally and spiritually.

There was a rap concert where the popular rapper had the whole crowd going crazy, and there was a man sitting in the front row not clapping or standing up. The rapper sang several more of his most popular songs; the crowd was in a frenzy, but the guy in the front row still sat there not clapping, standing or dancing. The rapper got so frustrated that in the middle of the concert he stopped singing and motioned to his band to stop playing. The audience, not knowing what was going on, thought this was a planned break. The rapper, in front of thousands, began to rebuke the spectator in the front row. This went on for a couple of minutes. After his tirade, the band started up again and the rapper continued with an edge. Later, he found out that the man was mentally challenged and disabled! He couldn't stand, sing, clap or dance, but he wanted to be there to hear the music of his favorite rapper. I feel that many would stand up and dance in church, if they could, but they can't!

In an orphanage setting, with all these children and all these needs, uniformity is essential so the leadership can handle the masses and the church runs smoothly. In the Romanian orphanages they would isolate the problem children (the nonconforming ones) and tie them to their beds! It's sad that a child is considered problematic because he wants to play baseball for one day but every day everyone plays soccer, or because he's fed up with potatoes and gravy every day and just has had enough, so he throws a tantrum but no one has the time to talk him through it, so he is isolated or tied up. When he calms down he can join the rest, but the core issues still remain until the next blowup. This seems harsh, but the directors are doing their best.

In a milk-driven church it can be the same: individuality and being opinionated can be looked at as negative or considered rebellious. It's easier to run these people off than to spend hours working through all their personal "issues." The ambitious are also a "pain." They want to do more or change things, but for the sake of peace and quiet we shut them down with mundane tasks or tell them, "You need training" and "Go to this ministry training class in another city in a few months." Those who have ongoing issues with leadership, some of which are valid, find that their petitions are all in vain because the "problematic" are so few and there are hundreds in the church who agree with the structure and seem happy (milk is good!). They have a choice: conform or leave. When it comes to sin in the church, in most cases it's overlooked; most people in the fellowship know but do nothing. If the sin becomes public then leadership gets involved, but because of the lack of resources, they are getting involved with a person whom they barely know. The person is called to repentance yet might not have been in such a crisis if there was ongoing, preventative, personal care.

Once the high-maintenance kids are dealt with—the sinful, chronically weak, opinionated, individualistic and ambitious—what is left is a milk-dependent audience, obedient and conditioned to the rules and bylaws of the church. Then the masses can be moved through preaching from the pulpit, specialty classes, programs, counselors, retreats and conferences instead of through one-on-one brother or sister help, which just isn't there. Another dynamic is the constant "knee jerkiness" with new-ministry configurations, new monthly or annual themes or a new video or book for all to read, but after the hype of the new thing has died, the immaturity remains. A lot of activity, but when you stand back there are still so many that show up to all the meetings but inside feel lacking and still have a deep yearning for the intimate love of Jesus. To sum up, the overwhelming needs perpetuate this unhealthy structure. The leaders are doing their best, but sometimes your best isn't good enough!

Jesus came for the sick, but if a low-maintenance ministry was what Jesus wanted, he wouldn't have picked these apostles: Judas, the sinful and deceitful; Peter, the opinionated hothead; Thomas, the doubter and later Saul, the ambitious zealot. Jesus walked with the Twelve 24/7 for three years and never gave up on them, even when they gave up on themselves. If the ambitious are distracted and the opinionated and outwardly sinful have been chased off, all that's left are the numb, the oblivious and the cowardly (Revelation 21:8, a major sin of omission). At that point, one would have ministry compliance that works well if the twenty percent and staff are overwhelmed. With this type of church culture it's hard to find objectivity and different points of view because all the opinionated are gone. Would there be any wonder why no one aspires to be a leader? It's because those who are left are fed milk and are dependent on someone telling them what to do or they must adopt the pharisaical model that their successors must hold up the institutional laws before being promoted, even over caring for people and loving the truth.

The Bullied Orphan

When an institution becomes rigid in their thinking and paranoia has set in, that environment can become very dismissive and harmful. The Jews had a similar mindset. They became closed to new thoughts and opinions. God sent prophets and even his own Son to warn them of their inbred theology, but they persecuted or even put to death those that he sent. Nicodemus was so frightened of the institutionalized Jewish religion that he came to Jesus at night. Making sure no one saw him, he kept in the shadows. How sad that a full-grown man's fear of what his peers would think of him kept him in the shadows. He acted this way because he knew that Jesus' truth didn't fit the Pharisaical worldview. Nicodemus acted like a Jewish orphan, scared, paranoid that he'd be branded a heretic, and fearful of being kicked out of the Temple because his thoughts might be different.

Nicodemus had a moment of courage after his conversation with Jesus. He tried to bring up reason with his Jewish peers among the leaders and this happened:

> *Nicodemus, who had gone to Jesus earlier and who was one of their own number, asked, "Does our law condemn anyone without first hearing him to find out what he is doing?"*
> *They replied, "Are you from Galilee, too? Look into it, and you will find that a prophet does not come out of Galilee."*
> —John 7:50–51

Nicodemus tried to bring up their own laws but got shut down by an outlandish statement about him being from Galilee, attempting to discredit Jesus not by what he said (the truth) but by where he was from. When we are holding on to something that is so fragile in what we believe or are doing, we will look for anything to discredit the one bringing it to the forefront: their age, their lack of time in the church, their lack of theological education or training, their poor attendance, their lack of advice-seeking, lack of giving, etc. Using this fear tactic, we can always find something to discredit anyone; this is one of the oldest childish (not childlike) ploys. Also, after this exchange of words with his peers, those who were looking on saw how Nicodemus was attacked and didn't speak up in his defense or for their law; they were cowards. This whole interaction shows an inbred culture of intimidation and shutting down differing views, hence not establishing a safe environment, and therefore people were keeping their thoughts in the shadows. These types of institutions are driven by fear and not by faith. Their passion and energy are spent defending their institutionalized beliefs by creating new laws, policies and programs instead of being in the trenches by loving God's children to maturity and developing a personal ministry.

Many religious institutions have tempered their brash behavior because of negative media exposure or internal unrest and even splits. They claim to be open to new thought and ideas but when one steps back and looks at the main leadership structure and how things are done, it's the same infrastructure that has been for the last twenty to thirty years. All of these institutions eventually burn out because they are blind to new thought and innovation in the Spirit, similar to what happened to the Pharisees. If one has the truth, it doesn't matter what is said or done, truth will always prevail (Mark 13:31). Those who don't believe this principle will do anything to protect their perceived truth with fear and intimidation. Love and fear cannot coexist! *"There is no fear in love. But perfect love drives out fear, because fear has to do with punishment. The one who fears is not made perfect in love"* (1 John 4:18).

Spiritual Abuse

We constantly hear about emotional, mental or physical abuse but not spiritual abuse. I have heard it said that it is easier to heal from a physical beating than from ongoing emotional abuse; we can be psychologically scarred for life. How about from spiritual abuse? Even in the church, the spiritual epicenter, I don't hear people say they have been spiritually abused. If we can't see it, how can we say it? Could we be unconsciously hurting each other spiritually and not know it? But many in all denominations are feeling unheard, guilt-driven, neglected or unloved, bullied into conformity like

Nicodemus, overcoddled by someone else thinking for them, or lacking empowerment like Terry. All of these things, over time, will suck the joy and confidence out of any child. How do I know? These beaten-down orphan believers, including ministry staff, are in my counseling office. The greater travesty, however, is that they have to pay a stranger for objectivity because of the closed-mindedness and lack of empathy in their own church community. So sad!

When one is hurt in the church, the pain is multiplied tenfold compared to in the world. We come into the church with the promise of a safe place for childlikeness, and we believe it. In the world we have our guard up and we get to a point that we don't trust anyone. In the church, the walls come down, so when we are hurt by misunderstanding, someone's yes being no, gossip, someone sinning against us or leadership hypocrisy, there is no defense. We are devastated! This spiritual abuse and the resulting hurt sends us reeling, and now where can we go when we feel the church has failed us? The problem is that the sins mentioned are all man-related, and man will always fail you. But the loving Dada is always there.

When a milk-driven church makes it more about the structure in their attempts at moving the masses through leadership and laws, there will always be waves of unrest because people deep down will not be happy, and there will be splits over the silliest things because they are man-made minutia and not of the Father's love. Through this love one would find more grace and forgiveness for all. As children of God, we are sensitive and fragile. Jesus understood this and referred to his disciples, who were full-grown men, as children. He went to great lengths to reassure them, creating a nurturing environment where conflicting views were welcomed and his disciples constantly expressed openly their thoughts without condemnation, making it a safe, loving place. Jesus valued everyone's individual feelings, which we will see in the next chapter, and gave them free will to be what the Father wanted them to be. The question I have is, how did Jesus deal with this orphan mindset?

Chapter 19

Jesus' Orphans

"I will not leave you as orphans."

—Jesus, in John 14:18

How can anyone feel like an orphan around Jesus? To his apostles who had been around him for three years, Jesus said, "I will not leave you as orphans." Jesus knew that his ministry structure perpetuated immaturity and that his disciples didn't understand the cross even though he had explained it to them several times; they had spiritual amnesia. His disciples were too dependent on milk from him and needed some radical changes to grow to the next level.

John spends four chapters in his gospel telling how Jesus reassured their orphan fears. We will be examining scriptures from chapters 13–16 (all with emphasis added).

The Fear of Being Left Alone

*"Because I have said these things, you are filled with **grief**"* (16:6).

*"Do not let your hearts be troubled and do not be **afraid**"* (14:27).

*"**My children, I will be with you only a little longer.** You will look for me, and just as I told the Jews, so I tell you now: Where I am going, you cannot come* (13:33).

One of the greatest fears is loneliness. Many will go to great lengths to not feel alone with their thoughts and insecurities. Jesus' disciples were no different. Their superhero was leaving. With the right encouragement, his disciples could walk on water and drive out demons, but at the thought of Jesus leaving them they were grief stricken. This perceived abandonment left them feeling spiritually orphaned. Three years previously they had left everything: their families, homes and careers; and they didn't have a plan B. But Jesus never lost sight of their childlikeness, referring to them as children, understanding that in their sensitive hearts they were acting that way. He didn't minimize their pain and tell them to suck it up and get over it; instead he spent the time helping them even though he had told them several times what he must suffer (John 5:25, 6:62, 7:33, 8:21, 10:17, 12:23–24, 12:35). Why were they so shocked? They had heard it from the mouth of Jesus again and again. Were they in denial or disconnected from the metanarrative of God? They were oblivious and spiritually numb to the realities of the salvation of mankind and the passion of Christ.

His Physical Departure

*Jesus replied, "Where I am going, **you cannot follow now**, but you will follow later." Peter asked, "Lord, **why can't I follow you now?** I will lay down my life for you" (13:36–37).*

*Thomas said to him, "Lord, we don't know where you are going, so **how can we know the way?**" (14:5).*

*Then Judas (not Judas Iscariot) said, "But, Lord, **why do you intend to show yourself to us and not to the world?**" (14:22).*

I do not give to you as the world gives (14:27).

We view everything in life from a tangible perspective, and this is how we define our reality. The thought is that having Jesus with me physically would help me be a better Christian. I would be so confident and bold! Even though the apostles had Jesus with them night and day for three years, they constantly doubted their abilities and giftedness. As Christians, we live in two worlds: the spiritual world and the physical world. The disciples wanted to physically go where Jesus was going, but the cross was for the spiritual redemption of mankind. After all this time with him they didn't see his ultimate spiritual calling. That's spiritual amnesia!

His disciples, with carnal vision, saw any physical pain such as the passion, as wrong. His apostles were willing to die to stop him from being arrested and taken to the cross, but Jesus was following the will of his Father. Many in the church pray that people be saved from pain and sickness, but there could be a greater cause. Despite his followers' carnal pleas, Jesus was resolute. He kept the greater good in front of him, wrestling with his flesh and God's will to the point of sweating blood in the Garden of Gethsemane. Through his death and resurrection he was ushering in a spiritual kingdom, which the humanistic and dependent—the Pharisees and his apostles at this time—wouldn't understand. So this question remains: What is better than being in the physical presence of Christ?

Jesus' Tough Love

> But I tell you the truth: **It is for your good that I am going away. Unless I go away, the Counselor will not come to you; but** if I go, I will send him to you (16:7).

As a father, I try to intentionally parent my kids; I must look at their characters and guide them to maturity. Sometimes I have to make tough decisions that will cause them discomfort to reach that next level of maturity. One of the reasons we moved from the USA to the UK was for our kids. They were eight and eleven at the time and were becoming ungrateful and spoiled. Sharisse and I didn't grow up this way and to this day we are appreciative of the little things. When we decided to sell everything it was an eye-opening experience for our kids, selling their stuff and only taking suitcase-friendly toys with them. From this, they now value the little things and are thankful for them. I view this as tough love. If we have a Father, and we are his kids, then surely he's doing the same in our lives. His goal is for us to be "mature and complete, not lacking anything"; then we can accept pain, sickness and the uncertainty of his will. Jesus, the son of God, understood the metanarrative of his Father and knew that leaving his apostles was for a greater good and for their greater maturity. This is the tough love of God.

Some questions: How do you view pain? Do you believe that our Father knows what is needed in your life or do you buck hardships when they come? Do all the t's need to crossed and the i's dotted before you do God's will? What happens to our character if we keep on avoiding conflict and hardship?

A Permanent, Loving Home

> Jesus replied, "If anyone loves me, he will obey my teaching. My Father will love him, and we will come to him and **make our home with him**" (14:23).

> "Do not let your hearts be troubled. Trust in God; trust also in me. **In my Father's house are many rooms**; if it were not so, I would have told you. I am going there to **prepare a place for you**" (14:1–2).

As a young child I never had my own room. When we lived in London, we lived in a one-bedroom flat where my mum and dad slept on the pull-out couch in the living room and the three kids slept in one small room together. The place had no bath or shower; my mum bathed us in the old-fashioned ceramic sink. Amen, Jesus is preparing a place for us; finally, as a child (of God), I get my own room! The greatest challenge for orphaned children is, will they find a loving home? Growing up as an interracial kid, rejected by both sets of grandparents, there were times I felt I didn't belong and would ask myself, "Where is my place in this world?" Today, I don't lose hope because my loving Father has a family of all colors and races waiting for me in heaven. Many of us are struggling in our current situation, be it with health, choices, family, work or marriage, and life has not worked out the way we had planned. I want you to take courage that one day all this will pass. Our loving Father has that one covered; he has an eternal home that will never close its doors to his faithful children. In my life I have moved homes more than twenty times, I have been homeless, slept on strangers' floors, and as a child been startled awake in the middle of the night, having to leave in a hurry because we were being evicted. As a teen, I locked myself in my room to shut out the domestic chaos. Now I find strength in knowing there is a loving, stable and peaceful dwelling. Brothers and sisters, we must push on to that eternal place that we all can call home once and for all, a true homecoming.

I Am No Longer with You But in You!

> *The world cannot accept him, because it neither sees him nor knows him. But you know him, for he lives with you and **will be in you*** (14:17)

> *On that day you will realize that I am in my Father, and you are in me, and **I am in you*** (14:20).

I'm going to be in you! Is this some alien abduction? No, Jesus is talking about the indwelling of the Holy Spirit (Acts 2:38). Jesus had to leave so the Holy Spirit would be present in our hearts and minds. When you are in love and you want to spend 24/7 together, how about having that person inside your heart? You would never feel alone. You would always have someone to talk to and someone there in all situations to give you advice and guide you. When it comes to the Holy Spirit it's like Jesus is always with me because he's in me. That's better than him being next to you. Do you believe this?

> *And we rejoice in the hope of the glory of God. Not only so, but we **also rejoice in our sufferings**, because we know that suffering produces perseverance; perseverance, character; and character, hope. And hope does not disappoint us, because **God has poured out his love into our hearts by the Holy Spirit**, whom he has given us.*
>
> —Romans 5:2b–5, *emphasis added*

Now through your "orphan moments" at 1 a.m. in the eerie darkness of your bedroom or at 3 p.m. in the manic pace of your workplace, you don't have to panic and look around for Jesus for reassurance but can look inside. Our Dada poured HIS love into our hearts; just turn on the Holy Spirit tap and let his love and comfort wash out all your doubts, all your insecurities and all your fears. That's refreshing and liberating! That's why Jesus had to go: he understood his limitations of being in the flesh. Preachers, pastors, elders, counselors and discipleship partners all have human limitations, but the Holy Spirit can reassure you anytime, anywhere and in all situations.

The Power Within

> And I will ask the Father, and he will give you another **Counselor to be with you forever—the Spirit of truth**. The world cannot accept him, because it neither sees him nor knows him. But you know him, for **he lives with you and will be in you**....
> But the Counselor, the Holy Spirit, whom the Father will send in my name, **will teach you all things and will remind you of everything I have said to you**. Peace I leave with you; my **peace I give you**.
> —John 14:16–17, 26–27, *emphasis added*

Having the indwelling of the Holy Spirit equips you better than any man or even Jesus could in the flesh. The Holy Spirit has been around since the beginning of time. He was there when God spoke the world into creation. Having him inside of you, he will guide you in all truth, reminding you of what Jesus said and did. He is the Counselor and fills you with wisdom beyond your age. The Spirit is the equalizer and anyone who is indwelled with him deserves to be listened to, from a teen to someone in their eighties. I see in many churches where it's about theological degrees, who you know and how long you've been around, but the Holy Spirit gives the youngest Christian a voice. If godly wisdom can come from a donkey (Numbers 22:27–30) with the Spirit, it can come from us!

Chapter 20

The Spirit Cries Out!

*For those who are according to the flesh set their minds on the things of the flesh, but those who are according to the Spirit, the things of the Spirit. **For the mind set on the flesh is death, but the mind set on the Spirit is life and peace**, because the mind set on the **flesh is hostile toward God**; for it does not subject itself to the law of God, for it is not even able to do so, and those who are in the **flesh cannot please God**. However, you are not in the flesh but in the Spirit, if indeed the Spirit of God dwells in you. But if anyone does not have the Spirit of Christ, he does not belong to Him.*

—Romans 8:5–9 NASB, *emphasis added*

What is your mindset on the flesh and the Spirit? There is no middle ground; we are either living in the flesh or in the Spirit. Even though we have the Spirit, he can be oppressed by humanism (the flesh). If the Spirit is not the ultimate driving force in our lives, reflected in our mindset, we are living ineffective lives. Flesh-led ministry is predictable, with its annual retreats, classes and programs, but the Spirit is not. Again, we can't be corporate and of the Spirit! Flesh-driven ministry leaves us numb, oblivious to the needs of others and their lostness. Fleshers look outward for revelation or a fix in the form of books, classes or the next big thing, just like orphans constantly in want and feeling inept.

In contrast, when we read the Acts of the Apostles (really the acts of the Holy Spirit), every day was different; the Spirit led the Christians to God's will. A church should be a gathering of those inspired by what God is doing in their lives. When everyone is expressing their individual giftedness for the greater good of the collective, that's church. Each one is empowered by the Holy Spirit to be Christlike and is constantly changing because they are being convicted by his working inside of them (John 16:8). No one needs to tell them once they are plugged into God's Spirit (the Holy Counselor); they already know or know better.

With King David, the man after God's own heart, God had to send Nathan to confront him on his sin and involvement in Uriah's murder. David had gone a year stewing in his sin and guilt; he had severed himself from God's Spirit, and Nathan's rebuke was his only spiritual lifeline left. When someone has to tell you that you are doing wrong, it's the last resort, not the first! One must disengage the Holy Spirit, their conscience and their knowledge of Scripture to continue in their hardhearted folly. We have to be devoid of spiritual sensitivity for the sin to be so full blown that anyone can see it and then intercede (James 1:13–15).

My wife was having a tea time with some ladies who had known each other from the same church for more than twenty years. They later discussed who else could join their spiritual tea time, and the ladies brought up several names. They stopped at one name and said she was selfish and spoke about her for several minutes, during which the "selfish" label came up again and again. My wife interjected with, "Does this woman know that she's selfish?" and they were silent! My wife insisted, "If she doesn't know it, then you are gossiping about your spiritual sister and you need to tell her in love." They apologized to my wife, a practical stranger in their lives. It's sad to see people around each other for many years (in this case, at over 1,000 church services) and not loving each other enough to point out what they see. Because of their fleshly thinking they were oblivious of their gossip and lack of love for their sister. This "selfish" sister could have been set free years ago with just a few words of encouragement.

Telling them is the first step, but unless they reengage with God's Spirit, you will be having the same conversation in a couple of months. Anyone can make a humanistic rally for a few weeks, but the

Spirit heals, empowers and sustains.

> *For all who are being led by the Spirit of God, these are **sons** *of God**. For you have not received a spirit of **slavery leading to** *fear again**, but you have received a spirit of adoption as sons by* *which we cry out, "**Abba! Father!**" The Spirit Himself testifies* *with our spirit that we are children of God, and if children, **heirs*** *also, heirs of God** and fellow heirs with Christ, if indeed we suffer* *with Him so that we may also be glorified with Him.*
> —Romans 8:14–17 NASB, *emphasis added*

Throughout this book we have been on a journey to fill a spiritual and emotional void using scriptures about our Father's promise that we are no longer homeless, are not orphaned and are no longer fatherless but are loved sons and daughters of God. Also we are heirs and benefactors of a heavenly promise. We can now be set free of the slavery of fear, and in jubilation the Holy Spirit cries out, "*Abba*, Father"!

What a release! One can't hold it in. We cry out "*Abba*" because finally we have found the answer to that paternal hole in our hearts. We cry out "*Abba*" because it's an end to all the fruitless pursuits. We found our affirmation, our love and our safe place we have longed for. We cry out "*Abba*" because we finally repented (turned back), reversing adulthood back to childhood. The Holy Spirit cries "Dada," Jesus cries "Dada" in the Garden of Gethsemane and our first words are "Dada." We all cry, "*Abba*, Father"!

Superpowers for All

Well, girls and boys, children, we started this journey with my story of my Batman costume. What we love about our superheroes is that they live ordinary lives but in the time of need they have superpowers. As Christians we are indwelled with a timeless superpower, the Holy Spirit, but how powerful is he?

> *And if the Spirit of him who raised Jesus from the dead* *is living in you**, he who raised Christ from the dead will also **give*** *life to your mortal bodies through his Spirit**, who lives in you…* *because those who are led* by the **Spirit of God are sons of God**.…

*Now if we are children, then we are heirs—heirs of God and co-heirs with Christ, if indeed we share in his sufferings in order that we may **also share in his glory** (Romans 8:11, 14, 17, emphasis added).*

Yes, the power that is in you is the same power that can raise the dead (Jesus)! I will say it again: the same power that raised the Son of God after three days in the tomb is living in you! Superman had to reverse the world's rotation to raise Lois Lane from the dead, but our Father has a way for us to tap into his power. I see so many in the church who have little understanding of what the Spirit can do and are constantly looking outward for illumination, but all our spiritual answers are inside where lives the Holy Counselor who will lead us to all truth. This principle goes against all our humanistic schooling and logic. We must detach ourselves from our flesh and unleash the Spirit of God (Rom 8). It's like living a riding lawnmower life, putting along, when there's a V12 Lamborghini engine inside roaring to come out. We have superpowers to overcome the basic temptations and woes of this world. We don't live a mere mortal existence but a glorious supernatural one!

Earlier we read about orphaned Terry, grieving over the man he used to be. When we met that evening, I could have beat-him up with his sin and what he wasn't doing in the church. But as an orphan he was already downtrodden, so why should I beat him down any more? We had only one conversation, and it was painful but in a tough loving way. My prayer was that he felt my love and encouragement but all the more his Dada's love. I focused our conversation on the Holy Spirit that God had instilled in him and the superhero greatness that was inside of him. About a week later he sent me this email:

Marvin,

Hope things are going very well for you guys.

I really enjoyed seeing you at the conference. Our conversation was a blessing. God used you. Your words convicted me and I immediately wanted to repent [turn back] and think how can I live for Jesus every day. Those words from God have stuck with me and inspired me to be passionate for him and to make an impact.

God has used me and Cindy to encourage the church that He is with us and wants us to share the gospel in our surrounding towns. We shared at this past midweek's service. God has really renewed my heart since our conversation. Thank you for loving me enough to help me.

Love, Terry

Terry, like Morpheus in *The Matrix*, fought the lies of the evil agents who tried to fill his mind with fear and hopelessness. Terry believed in the promise and power of God and broke the chains of mundane living and unbelief. This orphan saw his loving dada and broke out of the orphanage of fear, guilt and lies.

He and his wife are reengaged with Dada's Spirit and now you can't stop them. Over the last two years they have seen several neighbors and family members become Christians. They are superheroes with superpowers—the Holy Spirit and the love of Jesus—saving the fatherless from the evil woes of this world.

Questions: How often do you think about the power inside you? Are you living a lawnmower or a Lamborghini life? Do you believe you can change this quickly? What's stopping you from tapping into your greatness?

Chapter 21

Dearly Loved Children

There is an orphan child in all of us. Despite everything that has happened to me and my wife through our lives, we don't feel like victims. No, we feel empowered to help others, hence me writing this book. We are empowered because our Father's love trumps the neglect, the beatings, the sexual molestation, racism, poverty, homelessness, abandonment and poor parental role models in our lives. The scriptural inspiration for this book is *"Be imitators of God, therefore, as **dearly loved children** and live a life of love"* (Ephesians 5:1, *emphasis added*).

Being a loved child lays a foundation of security and empowerment. Unfortunately, I did not have this upbringing, and many reading this have had some of the same experiences. My life, without a father's presence, was like having a stone in my shoe and every now and then it would dislodge itself from the space in the toe and send excruciating pain through my body. No matter where I went or who I was with, it was always there. You can be at the happiest place in the world and that little orphan pebble is lurking in a dark crevasse of your soul (sole) waiting to derail that moment. There was a rift between me and my father for most of my life. I thought that moving 5,000 miles from the UK to the USA would help remove that stone but it did not, and neither did alcoholism. After ten years of running with a stone in my shoe, my foot was a bloody mess. Until I faced my hurt and myself, then and only then could I finally take out the stone and heal. I could then walk the life that God had ordained for me (phew! no more running).

Today, I have compassion for my parents and tell them that I love them because I feel loved. Hurt people hurt people and loved people love people! Many have based their love on how people treat them, so their love goes up and down depending on how they feel. When you feel the consistent love of the Father, it's like an overflowing well that bubbles over into other people's lives. Yes, people still hurt me, and I get frustrated with my kids and my wife, but I go back to my Father for solace and reassurance. Then I can get up and love again. I am able to cast my anxieties on him and see things from an eternal perspective. To be honest, I feel more confident now than ever, because I truly feel God's love. My heavenly Father has filled the void that my parents did not or were unable to. In spite of my reckless adolescence for twenty-five years of my life, I feel content and am medication- and alcohol-free. I have surrendered my bitterness, my victim mindset, my rage and my sense of abandonment.

I thank God that I am bringing up my kids with more love than I received and that they will be able to live more heroic lives than I. They are confident because they feel love; they feel that they can walk on water. We are not perfect parents and my kids will be first to say it, but we strive to build a safe and loving home. I want my kids to know that they have a loving home to come back to so when they go out and need a plan B to heal and to reassess, or if they just need a loving hug, our door and hearts will always be open.

As I write this, my daughter is 500 miles away at camp with no immediate way to contact me (camp rules: no cell phones, a teen's nightmare!). Even though she can't see me or contact me, she is having the time of her life with her friends, fueled by the reassurance that her mother and father love her deeply. She can't see us but she feels our love.

Although we can't see our Father in heaven, we can still feel his love. When you have a loving Father, someone who will always listen, always comfort and always reassure, when man fails you, you can confide in him and heal in his loving arms. If you are alone without a love in your life, he is there; if you are going through a situation that no one understands, he understands; if you have health issues and you sit there in pain, he comforts you because he is in you. We are dearly loved children of God.

Empowered to Live a Life of Love

"Be imitators of God, therefore, as dearly loved children and live a life of love." When a child of God understands their Father's unfailing love and truly connects with the Holy Spirit, they are an unstoppable force. The Holy Spirit empowers ordinary people to do extraordinary things. One story is that of Philip, who waited on tables. Through the direction of the Holy Spirit, Philip took the gospel out of Judea to Samaria, which the apostles were told to do by Jesus in the Great Commission but didn't. The Holy Spirit went on to use Philip to meet the Ethiopian eunuch, who in turn took the gospel to Africa when up until this time the church had been only in Jerusalem.

When we look at the apostles, they were fishermen and blue-collar folk. They constantly struggled with Jesus' purpose and death, as we saw in previous chapters. Even after his death and resurrection, Jesus found them in a fishing boat huddled up together like orphans, with no fish. They had gone back to the boat where he found them three years earlier (Mark 1:16–17), back to their fruitless worldly pursuits. Thomas still doubted and wanted to put his fingers in the holes in Jesus' wrists (gross!). When Jesus ascended to heaven they didn't seem that inspired to spread the gospel. The defining moment when everything changed was when the Holy Spirit came upon them. In one day 3,000 became believers, and the story continues through the book of The Acts of the Holy Spirit. These cowards, deserters, fallaways, these orphans, went on to martyrdom. The following are from *Foxe's Book of Martyrs:*

Peter (The Coward)

Jerome saith that [Peter] was crucified, his head being down and his feet upward, himself so requiring, because he was (he said) unworthy to be crucified after the same form and manner as the Lord was.

Paul (The Persecutor)

Paul, the apostle, who before was called Saul, after his great travail and unspeakable labors in promoting the Gospel of Christ, suffered also in this first persecution under Nero...the soldiers came and led him out of the city to the place of execution, where he, after his prayers were made, gave his neck to the sword.

Thomas (The Doubter)

St. Isidore of Seville's testimony: "This Thomas preached the Gospel of Christ to the Parthians, the Medes, the Persians, the Hyrcanians and the Bactrians, and to the Indians of the Oriental region and penetrating the innermost regions and sealing his preaching by his passion he died transfixed with a lance at Calamina, a city of India, and there was buried with honor."

A Father's love is not enough; we must be indwelled with the fearless and relentless power of the Holy Spirit to live superheroic lives. Now, the Trinity is complete: the Father's reassurance and protection, the internal wisdom and inspiration of the Holy Spirit and then comes the "life of love" like Jesus. Powerful and complete!

The Holy Spirit who empowered the apostles empowers us too. Superheroes will always give their lives to a greater cause, and there is no greater cause than standing for justice, fighting evil and saving people's souls from peril. As dearly loved children of God, we are empowered to live a life of love and impact.

Final Reflection

As I close, I reflect on the whole narrative of this book. It reminds me of my opening story of me as a little boy excited to save the world in my cheap plastic Batman mask and cape. That childhood desire is still as strong now at nearly fifty as it was at five; I want to make a difference in people's lives! Dada, how am I doing?

The child never dies!

Appendix I

10 Simple Things to Be Happy —Revisited

In this chapter, we will revisit the ten simple things to make you happy, according to science, that we first looked at in chapter two.

No matter what your nationality or beliefs, we all have the same struggles that stress us out: kids, work, health, relationships. I've travelled all over this wonderful world, and people are people. Even as an atheist, I reflected on some of these ten simple things, and I felt better when I did them. I remember doing unselfish acts (not many) and thought that someone would give me credit one day.

If we have a heavenly Father who created us as his children, he knows what makes us tick. He knows our inner thoughts and needs, and taking it one step further, he has neurologically wired us to live a joyful and full life, with boundaries and love for others. Science is only discovering what's been there since the beginning of time. As we examine again the ten simple things to make us happy, this time it will be from a spiritual perspective.

1. Be grateful
2. Get good sleep
3. Smile and be joyful
4. Be closer to family
5. Go outside
6. Arrange a shorter commute
7. Be active and exercise
8. Meditate or pray
9. Help others
10. Plan a trip

1. Be Grateful

As a dad, the number one thing to get my blood boiling is when my kids are ungrateful or complain about a gift. I would take it away because they were not thankful for it. So, coming to America from England, I was intrigued by US holidays, especially Thanksgiving, which has become my favorite (but July 4th I don't celebrate, for obvious reasons!). So, doing some research on Thanksgiving Day, it seems that President Lincoln was concerned that the American people were becoming ungrateful for the blessings bestowed on them, like naughty children.

Abraham Lincoln, 1863: Thanksgiving Proclamation

The year that is drawing toward its close has been filled with the blessings of fruitful fields and healthful skies. To these bounties, which are so constantly enjoyed that we are prone to forget the source from which they come, others have been added, which are of so extraordinary a nature that they cannot fail to penetrate and soften the heart which is habitually insensible to the ever-watchful providence of Almighty God.

No human counsel hath devised, nor hath any mortal hand worked out these great things. They are the gracious gifts of the Most High God, who while dealing with us in anger for our sins, hath nevertheless remembered mercy....

It has seemed to me fit and proper that they should be solemnly, reverently, and gratefully acknowledged as with one heart and one voice by the whole American people. I do, therefore, invite my fellow-citizens in every part of the United States, and also those who are at sea and those who are sojourning in foreign lands, to set apart and observe the last Thursday of November next as a Day of Thanksgiving and Praise to our beneficent Father who dwelleth in the heavens.

Many today would look back at those who lived in 1863 and consider them as though living in the Third World (no cars, no A/C, no smart phones, no electricity). President Lincoln was concerned in his day that America was becoming complacent and ungrateful, so he petitioned congress to make a day where a whole nation stopped and reflected on what they had. If we jump forward 150 years and if

Lincoln were alive and saw all the riches and materialism in the USA, he would not ask for a day of Thanksgiving, he would ask congress for a month! America has so much, but its citizens can be discontented and lack gratitude. If you live in the West you are so blessed compared to people in other countries. The poverty level here in the USA is $22,811 for a family of four, but in developing nations their criterion of poverty is their caloric intake per day, and two thirds of the world lives on less than two dollars a day (www.globalissues.org). But who decides where one is born? Who selects our parents? I could have easily been conceived by a couple in Somalia. Who decides this?

A Christian tenet is being grateful. Gratitude is essential to happiness. We can easily focus on what we don't have instead of what we have. As an atheist, the happiest time for me was Christmas because people were in a giving spirit and expressing goodwill to each other. Here's something that helps me and my clients: we put together a gratitude list of 100 things. The goal of this assignment is to lift your spirits and look at the glass as half full instead of half empty. We have been blessed with so much.

2. Get Good Sleep

Over 82 million (40%) U.S. adults and teens suffer from some type of insomnia.... As they age, it only gets worse. 54% of people over age 55 report sleeplessness once or more a week. Sleep deprivation costs $45 billion a year in lost productivity, health-care bills, and expenses related to traffic accidents, rivaling the impact of depression...or stroke.

BusinessWeek, 1/26/04

As we lay down our head in the darkness of the night, when the noise of life (screaming or demanding kids, deadlines at work and the general din of life) quiets, we are left with our overloaded consciences. Our past and present demons come out and play in the void between busyness and sleep.

A Christian principle is to reconcile and forgive. When someone says something that offends us, we brush it off and say it's no big deal although we are hurt. Our experiences of confronting people on their wrongdoings end with them becoming defensive and childishly turning the tables. No one likes confrontation and most of us just avoid it. Without healthy emotional boundaries the wrongdoing will continue, and after a few years of this our consciences are troubled so that late at night we lie awake bothered and restless.

As men, we act like we don't care and we have no feelings, but it catches up with us. Most men who were hard nuts when they were younger become weeping fools when they get older. I believe that every conscience has a limit to the amount of abuse and unresolved issues it can take and will reach critical mass leading to insomnia. Hence the studies show that people in their fifties have at least one or more sleepless nights a week. What's keeping them awake? It's the accumulation of unresolved issues, childhood abuses, missed opportunities and the hurtful and horrible things they said and did to others adding up and bubbling over into their subconscious. As this restless dynamic increases, one has to do something. Many turn to prescribed medications, weed smoking or alcohol.

As an adult, my substance of choice was alcohol. I needed to have four or five beers to numb my conscience to sleep, but deep down I was still troubled. When I was drinking at a bar or a club, the inner turmoil would boil over into arguing and sometimes full-blown fistfights with anyone over anything. The hurt inside of me was hurting others. So many demons to deal with and I didn't know where to start!

Our loving Father wants all his kids to get along. You have to start with yourself first, and after much study I made a decision to become a Christian and see if this "Father" had my back. I reconciled with many people I had hurt and asked for forgiveness for my selfishness. Since becoming one with my Father twenty-plus years ago, I can count on one hand my sleepless nights due to my conscience. Before then, alcohol, guilt-ridden insomnia and misery, but now I sleep like a baby. I feel like a child, and my Father tucks me in every night and wishes me a good night's sleep. How about you?

3. Smile and Be Joyful

Joy is different from happiness; some say that happiness depends on happenings, such as what you drive, how work is going, how people feel about you or how you feel about yourself. If we base how we feel on these factors we will live a yoyo life. Joy is an inner peace knowing God is in control. Joy is being content with what you have. It radiates from you and has a calming effect on others. When I was a child, I would be happy while playing with my friends. That was a distraction, but deep down I knew I had to go home to the mayhem. My happiness was always short lived because my home wasn't a safe place. There was laughter in my home but it was from making fun of each other through crude sarcasm, the hurt spilling over. Today, there is nothing more gratifying than as a father coming home to a house full of laughter and singing. It might not be in tune but it's a joyful noise. I want my kids to appreciate the inner joys of their childhood and be in a safe place.

4. Be Closer to Family

Most of this book has analyzed the effects of not being close to your family. We have examined what it's like to be homeless and to be emotionally or physically fatherless. If you haven't got this message by now, I have failed!

5. Arrange a Shorter Commute

Have a career that you love, but don't have a career that you love more than your spouse. You're not going to come to the end of your life and think, "I wish I'd spent more time at the office." Let work be a part of your life, not the entirety. Your spouse needs more from you than a financial contribution.

—Carrie Kitzmiller, catalogs.com

Spending too much time at work, including the commute, is one of the top ten things that kill a marriage and family (ask Rick who wrecked his car with me in it). When I've worked at Fortune 500 companies, many men could have gone home at 5 p.m. but they stayed until 7 or 8 p.m. because life at work was measurable but life at home was overwhelming. They would come home to a barrage of screaming babies or hormonal teens and exasperated wives. Work can become an escape to a controlled environment. This cycle continues, with the dads not knowing their kids and not knowing where to begin. Even on the weekends, Dad has his hobbies and complains that he needs his release from work. The marital frustration continues until it comes to a breaking point. When a marriage falls apart, the emotional shrapnel affects the kids too. In a strong marital relationship, the children have the best chance to grow up in a secure and safe environment. I've had clients in their forties who thought it was their fault that their parents split up because they were a bad five-year-old! That's sad, and these feelings have haunted them for decades. To make a relationship work, one must put the time in and be emotionally and physically available. God honors marriage and knows what is best for you and your kids. Some of us need to reevaluate our careers and priorities so as to leave no regrets in later life.

6. Go Outside

I've been confined to an office for several hours at a time. Getting outside and taking a breather is a refreshing break. If you are in the suburbs, you can see the trees and the stars at night. If we chill for a while, especially at night, we see the magnitude of the universe and realize we are a speck in the grand scheme of things. We can then see the complexity of things and how everything is intrinsically connected. In England people are concerned about the dramatic decrease of honey bees; initially I was dismissive and thought those people needed to get a life; what's next, the extinction of wombats? But doing more research I came to realize that honey bees are a big part of the pollination of plants and flowers, which affects our ecosystem. Every creature has an intricate part in making our planet work. None of this came about by a haphazard "big bang." Believing in the big bang theory is like believing that if you blow up a library with all its books and periodicals and fifty volumes of The Encyclopedia Britannica it will all fall back into some kind of order! Order can't come out of disorder—my childhood testifies to this.

I grew up poor, so my entertainment was always going out on the streets. It is sad that many kids outside of going to school don't go out. Their communication is reduced to Twitter, Facebook and texting smiley faces. The social skills of kids today are waning, which becomes a barrier to truly connecting with people, so that many don't have the relational fortitude to sustain a relationship when their feelings are hurt over a little misunderstanding.

Getting out and meeting people can be fun. One of the most exciting things is meeting someone you think you can be best friends with or be in a relationship with, that initial connection when you feel that you have much in common and have a similar worldview.

I'm writing this chapter in Starbucks, and sometimes I hit it off with a stranger coming in for a latte and we swap numbers. I am so excited by the possibilities of a new friend. Since we have moved so much they can be hard to come by. The emotional rush one gets from just dreaming of the possibilities of a best friend is so powerful. Most of these fledgling friendships go nowhere, but the continued search for that relationship or friendship keeps us going out.

There's an innate feeling of excitement we all get from a new relationship or friendship, and this is what the Father has instilled in us to live a life with others in an ever-increasing circle of friends. After family, friends are your plan C; the more true friends you have the more love and support you have in your time of need. I remember bringing my son to the kiddie park, where he would run up to another kid whom he had never met and they would start playing together, instant friends. Children keep it simple and keep trusting and building friendships. Happy kids have lots of friends.

7. Be Active and Exercise

As I've gotten older, it's been harder to keep the weight off, especially when my metabolism is grinding to a halt. I used to work in the health and fitness business and I would look down on those who were obese. I still work out to fight the bulge. I do a lot of public speaking, and I don't want people to discredit what I say by how I look. So it's important for me to stay in good health and especially with two active kids. When I feel the bulge is winning I get depressed; it's true that my physical condition affects my emotions. When we feel good about ourselves, that spirit touches others. We should all strive for holistic health: physical, mental, emotional and spiritual.

8. Meditate and Pray

> *Meditate: focus one's mind for a period of time, in silence...for religious or spiritual purposes or as a method of relaxation.*
> —The Oxford Dictionary

Meditation and prayer: for both to be effective, one must empty one's mind to connect. Twenty minutes of prayer and/or meditation can calm the cognitive noise, allowing you to get off the hamster wheel of life. We need time to center ourselves and have an outlet to express our feelings. Most women feel a lot, but when they bring out what's on their heart they feel better. Nothing has been said in return but they feel free through confession and openness. Prayer can have the same affect. When I was homeless and desperate, I prayed. I had already tried everything else! Even though I didn't believe initially, I do feel that God answered that prayer to save me from myself by putting a total stranger in my life to help me. I had used many people before this and wasn't grateful but rather felt entitled to it. This act of benevolence changed my life.

Sometimes our heavenly Father needs to see that we are serious and desperate for him to work in our lives. It's the same with my kids; they need to ask or really want something if they are going to get it. My kids have a lot of emotional whims, but if they persist with what they really want, then I may help them fifty percent of the way to get it. The goal is building character and making them appreciate the things they get. Through my counseling I have helped many who couldn't afford my services, yet I was willing to work with them to get them the help needed. I have found that if I offer my services for free, people don't show up and are ungrateful. However, if it has cost them something, they arrive on time, fully engaged in the process. In the same way a good father will find the balance of gratitude and blessing. Our heavenly Father is a blessing that anyone can tap into, for we are all his children. Unfortunately, like me, many don't call out to him unless we have to! Meditation and prayer calms our neurotic activity; science has even proven this. Try twenty minutes of nothing; many find this hard to do.

9. Help Others

The Terman study, which is covered in The Longevity Project, found that relationships and how we help others were important factors in living long, happy lives:

We figured that if a Terman participant sincerely felt that he or she had friends and relatives to count on when having a hard time then that person would be healthier. Those who felt very loved and cared for, we predicted, would live the longest.

Surprise: our prediction was wrong... Beyond social network size, the clearest benefit of social relationships came from helping others. Those who helped their friends and neighbors, advising and caring for others, tended to live to old age.
—Belle Beth Cooper, blog.bufferapp.com

As a dad, it's a constant emphasis with my children to be considerate of others and help people when the need arises. It is one thing to ask them for help, but when they help without being asked they are becoming naturally aware. Sometimes it seems like two steps forward and one step back. Our natural default is to be selfish; we must have a desire greater than ourselves to change our character and become selfless, be it from falling in love, being moved by compassion, having a child or a sick loved one, or wanting to watch over siblings.

A Christian ethos is always about helping others and the poor. Because of Christianity we have organizations like The Salvation Army, United Way and Red Cross. Any time there's a major natural disaster, these organizations are on the front line. In 2003, my wife and I volunteered during Hurricane Katrina for United Way and helped several hundred who were displaced. Also, hospitals and senior care centers were founded on the love of Christ. Compassion came into this world through Jesus. Do an historical study and you will find that before the first century the world was barbaric and heartless. The poor, elderly and mentally challenged were disregarded and left for dead. Something must have happened to change this course in history. Do you know of Muslim or Hindu global charities? No, this started with Christ. Our Father knows the things that make us happy, and one of them is helping others. It doesn't matter if you are a Christian or not, you feel the same; the scientific data shows this! Our heavenly Father has wired us to help others and live for others. He wants us to be happy just like any father wants their children to be happy.

10. Plan a Trip (The Final Destination)

The excitement of going somewhere on holiday makes us happy. Unfortunately, the trip or vacation often doesn't go exactly as planned, but it was still fun to plan. There is an ultimate destination we all have heard about where there is no more sorrow, tears or pain. It's heaven! Did you know that seventy-four percent of Americans believe in heaven (USA Today)? Even at pagan or nonbelievers' funerals they say they are in "a better place" or "at peace now." I've been to a few funerals where I knew the person had lived a selfish life, neglecting their wife and kids, but I still heard "He's in a better place"! As a minister, I've seen many people in their last days and seen the dread in their eyes and the uncertainty of the outcome of their lives. If they were going to die and end up as dust, what's all the angst about! Even the staunchest unbeliever leaves with fear and uncertainty. Even in my darkest hour as an atheist, I felt my good deeds would be credited to me in some form or some way. If we all knew our ultimate destination is heaven, we would live this life differently. I wouldn't be unchildlike, taking this life so seriously, and would be more concerned about my preparation for the trip to this final destination. Children live for today and live life out to the fullest.

I have a friend, Cletus, who a few weeks ago went to his doctor and was told he had bad indigestion. The pain increased, so he then went to a specialist who said the same and gave him a prescription medication. A couple of weeks later, Cletus couldn't eat and went to the emergency ward; after X-rays he was diagnosed with stage four cancer! The cancer was so aggressive that it was in his lymph nodes, his lungs and bone marrow. He can't eat anything but chicken broth and he's in a bad way, but the doctors are optimistic (they have to be!). I spoke to him yesterday and he was on the way to have a titanium rod put between his left knee and hip because they found cancer in his bone marrow so his leg could collapse at any time. After three chemo sessions, numerous exploratory surgeries and the doctors' mishaps, his spirit was upbeat and he prayed that God will be glorified through him. In our previous conversations he was more concerned about his wife and kids and their lives than his own. If Cletus passes away tomorrow, he will be at peace and ready for his final destination. He's a child of God and excited to leave this plane to be with his loving Father. What a homecoming!

I hope that this book has opened your mind to some new realities and led you to a place of childlikeness. Never stop learning and never stop being open to new relationships and understanding that your Dada wants the best for you.

Appendix II

Mission Update: An Adult to a Child

2008 was a great year for me: I graduated and attained my master's degree, wrote my first book and spearheaded a worldwide conference with fifty-five countries represented, where the keynote speaker was from Burma (this took three years to plan). Many would consider this a banner year, as I had reached the "adult" mountaintop experience of academia and recognition, but once the degree was framed and mounted, the book was published and the Burmese had gone back to Burma, I was uninspired and unfulfilled. Outside of these major events, my life was predictable: each year for eighteen years, the same calendar of meetings, events and conferences. Materialistically, we owned our home, the first in our family; we had finally gotten out of debt; we had two cars and we were living the American dream, considering both of us grew up poor. What was next? I could go back to school for my doctorate or plan another conference (more activity) but I wasn't doing well inside. Sometimes we have to stop the busyness of life to listen to the Spirit of God. I had this undercurrent of frustration in my life and I couldn't put my finger on it. There were times when I would come home and rant about someone or something and I couldn't let it go. My wife became very concerned and we would pray for peace in my heart. What was wrong with me? Looking back now, I believe it was that the child of God was dying in me!

By the end of 2009, I was at the breaking point, and after several conversations I decided to put in our resignation in February 2010. Many thought I was crazy at forty-six to quit a successful career, but I knew if I stayed in this spiritual state I would become numb and disenchanted. We had no plan B and didn't know where to go, but I didn't want to stay here. In one of the worst recessions in decades, we had no plans, no severance, no savings, no prospects; all we could do was pray! It reminded me of my time being homeless, totally helpless like a small child and at God's mercy. I wasn't fearful, because deep down I felt this was right spiritually, and since there is a loving Father orchestrating things for one's spiritual and emotional betterment, something would work out. Also, as a Father, he will look at my heart and my character and will do what is needed to deepen our Father and child of God relationship (Marvin, be careful what you pray for?). After many easier doors closing and only one tough one left open, we decided to sell everything and go to the UK to start a church in my hometown, the UK's most irreligious place. Once we got past passport control, we had no permanent place to stay, no jobs, no ongoing funding, just our Dada!

I felt that through this process of entrustment, I became truly dependent on God; I became a child again as my Dada came through again and again. Here are a couple of examples: at the end of several months when we didn't have our rent, a donation or a client came through; when our car broke down we were given another one; we had no furniture, and a relative stranger stepped forward in the church and furnished our house for us, including some antiques too. I can go on and on about my Father's ongoing deliverance in our lives. As an adult, I had all my safety nets in place: my salary; my retirement; my health, life, car and house insurances, and my savings; I didn't need God and my spirituality reflected that! I had to let go of my adult safety nets and let my Father catch me, which he did every time. One will never feel the full love and protection of their Father unless they truly feel they need him. OK, I sold everything and went abroad, but to be honest, this is nothing considering our fellow brothers in Christ were thrown to lions or impaled. God's plan for you could be something totally different but his refinement process is the same for all: *"Anyone who falls on this stone will be broken to pieces; anyone on whom it falls will be crushed"* (Matthew 21:44).

If you understand this principle, you either volunteer yourself to be broken or you will be crushed! I understood that my Father wanted to do great things in my life other than academics and event planning, but I had to put myself on the stone. From a worldly perspective, my decision was crazy and now I had broken our future to pieces, jeopardizing our retirement, career opportunities and savings. But my choice was a lot less painful than being crushed, especially when you least expect it. Due to all the coddling by physical family and church, and the safety nets we rely on, our response to the crushing is a childish one because of our underdeveloped character: playing the victim, anger, sulking and blaming others. If we don't put ourselves on the stone, we are left with the tough love of God to refine us to be like his Son. Here are some scriptures to emphasize this point:

> *Perseverance must finish its work so that you may be mature and complete, not lacking anything....*
> *Blessed is the man who perseveres under trial, because when he has stood the test, he will receive the crown of life that God has promised to those who love him.*
>
> —James 1:4, 12

There Are No Spoiled Kids in Heaven

Our Father's goal for us is to be with him for eternity, and he will use our circumstances to refine us so we can get there. If we don't give him much room to develop us due to our avoidance of suffering (Romans 5:3–5), he has to work through other avenues such as our health, family and kids. Let's look at how he can use our kids to develop us: if they are under the age of spiritual personal accountability and something tragic happens to them, their souls go back to the Father but we are left grieving, broken and in need of God's comfort. He weeps with us too (John 11:33–36). If this brings you closer to God and breaks the humanistic safety nets, it's a win/win to him because both you and the child will end up together in heaven for eternity. My advice is to throw yourself on the rock. It's painful and it will break you, but our loving Father will help you pick up the pieces and make you truly whole, that is, totally dependent on him.

This appendix was going to be about our journey back to my hometown and starting a church there and all the souls that were saved, and yes, that all happened (go to norwichchurch.org). But in reflection, I believe the ultimate mission here was to save me from the numbing effects of "adulthood" by letting my loving Father resuscitate childlikeness in my heart and mind.

After four years in the UK, we moved back to the USA, but as the saying goes, the "Lord giveth and the Lord taketh away." We left our car and furniture to a newlywed couple who needed the help to start their married lives. We had arrived with nothing and we left with nothing! Arriving back here in the USA, the blessing of the Father continued as we received another car (better than the one we left!) and our furniture was either given to us (even more antiques and china!) or bought in garage sales. Today, life is uncertain and we live on the edge financially but I wouldn't have it any other way; it keeps me from becoming complacent and dull. Spiritually, I feel alive and full of childlike aspirations, excited about my fiftieth year of life!

End Notes

1. Marvin Lucas, *Baguette Moments* (Spring Texas: Illumination Publishers, 2010).

2. Luke 15:11–32.

3. "Black Heart," written by Jo Perry, Shaznay Lewis, Iyiola Babalola and Darren Lewis (Warner Music UK, 2012).

4. Traci Bild, "The Day I Realized I Was No Longer the Woman My Husband Wanted," The Huffington Post, 10/15/2014.

5. Mohandas K. Gandhi, *The Story of My Experiments with Truth* (London: Penguin Books, 1987).

6. "The Logical Song," written by Rick Davies and Roger Hodgson (A&M Records, 1979).

7. Sharisse Lucas, *Because Life Happens* (Spring, Texas: Illumination Publishers, 2012).

8. Matthew 6:32–34, emphasis added.

9. Genesis 2:24.

If you enjoyed this book, please check out Marvin's first book *Baguette Moments* and also the book his wife Sharisse, wrote a book called *Because Life Happens,* both available at Illumination Publishers. Marvin has practiced counseling/ministry for twenty-years and had his own practice in Norwich England. In June 2014, he moved back to the states to pursue counseling, writing and ministry. He has spoken on this topic and others all over the world. You can contact him for any speaking engagements, or if you are interested in his counseling services by Skype, contact him at marvinlucas2@msn.com.

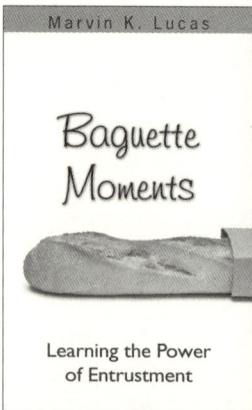

Marvin K. Lucas

Baguette Moments

Learning the Power of Entrustment

Both

available at

www.ipibooks.com

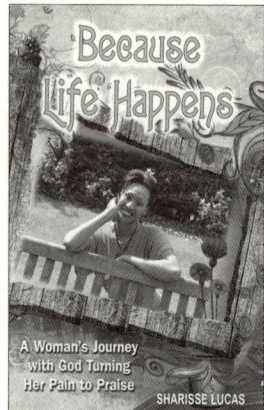

Because Life Happens

A Woman's Journey with God Turning Her Pain to Praise

SHARISSE LUCAS